Selecting For Success

THE FILMMAKER'S ART VOL. 2

Markus Innocenti

RED DOG LOGIC
LOS ANGELES, CALIFORNIA

Copyright © 2019 by Markus Innocenti.

All rights reserved. No part of this publication may be reproduced, distributed or transmitted in any form or by any means, including photocopying, recording, or other electronic or mechanical methods, without the prior written permission of the publisher, except in the case of brief quotations embodied in critical reviews and certain other noncommercial uses permitted by copyright law.

Statement of Fair Use

Some images of budget, scheduling and breakdown reports used to illustrate the author's viewpoints were created using commercially available production software, further information and example images of which are freely available on the open Web, as are any brief excerpts from published media content. The nature of this use is 'transformative' inasmuch as the underlying proprietary software or information used to create this original material repurposes the application, or material, in an educational and informative context (a) for an audience interested in filmmaking craft and techniques and (b) in a manner intended to add value by comparison, critique or comment. Material used has been strictly limited to achieve a transformative purpose only and the content creators, copyright owners and software product(s) have been appropriately credited.

'Silent Pictures: How First-Time Directors Think The Universe Is' © 2001 Katie Maratta. Used with permission. katiemaratta.squarespace.com
Book Layout & Design ©2013 — BookDesignTemplates.com
Cover Design — Red Dog Logic
Front Cover Photo from the Everett Collection, licensed through Shutterstock

Published by Red Dog Logic, an imprint of
Park Circle Limited, Glasgow, Scotland UK

ISBN 978-0-9986364-3-6

FOREWORD

Most screenwriters and film directors are people you've never heard of.

The famous ones, past and present, have always been the tip of a very large iceberg. Of those who do manage to make a regular living as a key creative, most remain anonymous to all but their immediate family and colleagues. A few of us don't even try to break the surface and become 'known' — but ego being what it is, those willing to toil without caring whether they are ever recognized or not are the exception.

I'm no different from most. After 35 years in the business, I'm still trying to write, direct or produce a film that — when I mention its title — most people will go, *'Oh, yeah, I saw that'*. So far, only my music videos have that distinction — but I'm still working on it. It's been a fun journey, even if the limo rides have been few and far between.

A while back I started thinking about what I've learned in my career. You get to the point where you want to pass something on, usually because what you're seeing, and hearing, is making you slap your own forehead too many times a day.

Let me share a secret. A few days before I directed my first full-length theatrical feature film, I realized that I'd never done this before, and I wasn't sure how I was going to get through the 30-day shoot. I had no real idea how to go about making a fiction drama. I was an experienced music video director, I'd made a couple of well-received 'shorts', produced a documentary, and I'd directed some commercials. On the basis of that, the executives and the agents and the star actors figured I knew what I was doing. I was in the solitary position of knowing that when it came to direct a theatrical feature — I didn't have a clue.

Nowadays, there's so much information on film-making, in particular on screenwriting and directing, you begin to wonder who's buying all these books and attending all those seminars. When I started out, there was nothing except William Goldman's entertainingly brilliant *Adventures in the Screen Trade* and *Truffaut/Hitchcock* — Francois Truffaut's massive interview with Sir Alfred. Other than that, you just had to figure it out from watching other people's work and trusting that you had a 'vision'.

So how did I get to this position of having producers, agents and stars believe that my business partner and creative collaborator, Edward Arno, and I were ready to take the leap into making what the contract specified as a 'First Class International Theatrical Feature Film'?

I'd been an actor for a while, but when people ask how I got started I tell them I entered the film industry in a truck — which is true. I had a job delivering grip equipment from rental houses to film sets. Most deliveries were for television commercial productions, but a few were for the big features. I had an epiphany one day after I'd brought some camera support equipment to Pinewood (a major studio outside London, England). I wandered onto the *Superman* (1978) set, the movie that made Christopher Reeve famous. I couldn't get over the size of the New York Street Exterior set — a massive façade for the 'Daily Planet' building where 'Clark Kent' and 'Lois Lane' worked. Looking at the activity, I began to understand more fully how the magic of film was mostly smoke, mirrors and a lot of painted plywood. I guess I got fired up because within five years I co-owned a stage and film production design company and was a union-accredited Art Director.

Everything in the film business is a small-step-by-small-step progress. There are seldom instant leaps. Eight years after that day on the *Superman* set, I was a music video director. Two years after that, and I was represented by one of the big agencies and signed to co-direct my first theatrical feature. And so there I was, just a few days before Principal Photography was due to begin, nervously realizing I hadn't actually directed a major long-form dramatic work before.

Most people who are even halfway good at anything tend to forget how hard and long the journey has been and how prepared they really are when the moment of truth arrives. They often think their success has been a fluke and that at any moment someone will pull back the curtain and expose their lack of talent. I was no exception. Gripped by a full-blown case of Imposter Syndrome I began to panic — until I remembered one of the first rules of success. If you don't know — ask. Even if, in asking, you risk making yourself look ridiculous.

I called author Steven Bernstein who'd recently completed what would become the best-selling *Film Production* (a standard student text from the moment it was published by Focal Press). Steven (who was on his way to becoming one of Hollywood's A-list cinematographers and a director in his own right) took ten minutes out of his day, told me to take a deep breath, reminded me that I'd already directed thousands of set-ups, and then proceeded to give me a step-by-step method of how to walk onto a feature film set and make it look as if I knew what I was doing. Steven Bernstein's generous insights gave me the knowledge and confidence to get through the first few hours on my debut feature without looking like a complete idiot, and since then I've built on that beginning.

Becoming a film director is no different from the learning curves and progressions made by artists working in any other of the creative arts or crafts. You start off a little unsure, a little hesitant and perhaps much too rigid in your own self-belief. Gradually, you learn how to do things the way they most often get done, you start to solve problems in ways that other artists have solved those problems before, and you feel your way towards the results you're looking for — most often with a large sense of dissatisfaction. Over time, like an improvisational jazz musician, you become so accustomed to your 'craft' and so adept at achieving your goal that you are able to apply your 'art' — the thing that distinguishes you from the others. The rules and rigidity no longer seem so necessary — but they are there to fall back on, the way a jazz musician knows the key, the mode and the scale that the musical structure relies upon.

The Filmmaker's Art series is designed to give you detailed basic knowledge that will allow you to step onto any movie set in the world and direct. From those essential basics — which every aspiring film-maker thinks they know, but actually don't — you will establish an acceptable 'craft' and a solid jumping-off point to start creating your own 'art'.

As I go through the series, I'll be looking to take you beyond the basics so that you can develop your own signature style. Bear in mind that my goal is to take you from 'craft' to 'art' in a business where 'art' often doesn't seem to count for very much — but is completely present in the work of the masters.

In *Decoding The Script*, the first volume in this series, I discussed how directors read scripts in ways that nobody else does, and how they identify elements within the script that will be overlooked by most readers, but which are vital to directing a film. *Selecting for Success* is designed to help you organize those elements and bring the script you have decoded into film production.

If you're already on your film-making journey, or even if you've yet to begin, some of what follows may seem obvious and already acquired. I hope you'll take a moment to allow those parts which might seem familiar to soak in completely and perhaps be reassessed.

Because even the greatest musicians sit down and practice scales now and again.

The best song you can write is the song that <u>only you</u> can write.

—RUPERT HINE

CHAPTER ONE

Choices

Let's imagine that you have agreed to direct a particular film project. You've read the script, you've had discussions with the Producer(s) and (perhaps) the Writer(s), you've been informed as to certain elements that are already in place — a Star Actor. A reliable Line Producer or Unit Production Manager. A 1st Assistant Director is already onboard. Perhaps, the preferred Cinematographer. You're excited to direct the picture — so you're not too worried about elements that arrived before you did. Not yet, anyway. You have negotiated your fee and your financial participation, should the completed film ever go into profit. You've been informed that Pre-Production will start next week, and that you will have six weeks to prep before Principal Photography begins. There is no firm Schedule as yet — but the idea being disseminated is that it can't be more than five weeks of shooting. There are different opinions as to whether those should be six-day or five-day weeks.

Oh — and the gentleman who invested $500,000 into your project and has been given the title 'Executive Producer' would like you to give his teenage daughter a significant role in the film.

For the purposes of the entire *Filmmaker's Art* series, I'm going to define the various levels of production budget according to how Contract Agreements have been made between Producers and the Screen Actors Guild (SAG). Similar arrangements exist worldwide, but I'll use the U.S. as a model. The Guild has four 'levels' of contract for feature films, each allowing a producer to work within a defined budget limit. These budget limits can be exceeded, in some cases, when producers decide to cast for diversity or hire SAG members as Background Performers ('Extras'). Please note that the comments that follow in italics/parenthesis are mine, not the Guild's, and are generalized observations).

Basic Theatrical. For films shooting worldwide with budgets over $2,500,000. (*Every studio picture, and almost all top-level independent feature films, employing internationally recognized 'name' talent*).

Low Budget. For theatrical feature films shooting in the US and budgeted under $2,500,000 (*Most "indie" films, employing domestically-known 'name talent' in key roles and perhaps a significant "international" name in a cameo*).

Modified Low Budget. For theatrical feature films shooting in the US with a budget not exceeding $700,000. (*Mostly, these are 'genre' pictures made by independent producers with track records — 'horror' predominantly — with up-and-coming, still-unknown talent in the youthful roles and "known" players in cameo roles*).

Ultra-Low Budget. ('ULB') For productions shooting only in the US, but with budgets under $250,000. (*This is the playground for emerging talent both in front of, and behind, the camera — with production largely funded by private investment, sponsorship and, in some cases, the 3 F's. (Friends, Fools and Family)*

SAG has also introduced two further contract levels designed (as were the Modified and the ULB agreements) to give producers of cost-conscious projects access to, and a means to hire, SAG members.

Short Project. Budget maximum $50,000, US production only, Total Running Time not to exceed 40 minutes.

Student Film. Budget under $35,000, TRT under 35 minutes, filmmakers to be students at an accredited institution.

To summarize; 'Low Budget' means a budget of $2.5m or less. There are two more distinctions within the 'Low Budget' category. 'Modified' with a ceiling of $700K, and 'ULB' maxing out at $250K. (Incidentally, The Directors Guild of America (DGA) defines 'Low Budget' to be under $2.6m — and that's a significant cut-off given the differential in fees and 'guaranteed' length of employment given to directors at the various scale levels.)

What about the much-vaunted 'Micro-Budget' you ask? Feature films with budgets from $5,000 to $50,000?

The short answer is that Micro-Budget production rarely uses, or can afford, SAG talent — and certainly can't afford a Union Crew. (At time of writing, the Theatrical Daily Rate for a Screen Actors Guild performer is — $985, Low Budget — $650, Modified — $350 and ULB — $125, plus Pension & Health benefits, (a.k.a 'Fringes'). These numbers are 'scale' — the base amount from where negotiation can begin. If you hear an actor say he'll work "for scale", that means he will accept the Guild minimum — but I digress.)

I'm going to keep 'Micro-Budget' in mind, of course, because it's a viable way to launch your career, but my focus in this book is really on the Ultra-Low Budget to Low Budget range. $250,000 to $2,500,000.

That's a lot of ground, but the interesting thing is that a Director should be approaching the directing tasks represented by these budgetary poles in exactly the same way. The ULB, Modified and Low Budget levels each have their own set of problems and pressures, but the way of working through those issues is similar.

I'll be assuming that the production will be shot digitally, (currently) using cameras like the ARRI Alexa LF or the RED Weapon/Monstro/Dragon/ models for the upper end of our budgetary ranges, cameras like the ARRI Amira, the Blackmagic Design URSA-Mini Pro 4.6K, and Canon's Cinema EOS series in the mid-point and — last but not least — inexpensive DSLR cameras (mostly Canon and Sony models) and iPhones at the lower 'Micro-Budget' end. I will sometimes discuss 'film' (meaning film stock formats of between 8 mm and 65 mm) — but will make sure that when I do, it will be clear I'm talking about film and film stock — as opposed to digital image capture.

Let it be said, however, that once you're over the $2.5m budget and enter the world of the Basic Theatrical Agreement you're in a different territory and a whole additional set of pressures will come into play, not least the executive oversight, massively increased logistics and the significant introduction of star talent — both in front of, and behind, the camera — working at an artistic level you might not have experienced before. Be assured and remain confident — there are many directors who have jumped from 'Micro-Budget'/'Low Budget' production levels and made their second or third picture for $40m or more. The same principles that a Director applies to direct a 'Low Budget' or a properly-helmed 'Micro-Budget' film stay true. The methodology is constant.

Think of it this way and take some comfort for your future. Francis Coppola directing a $15,000 production for Roger Corman is, I suggest, the same brain — and largely the same directorial skillset — as the Francis Coppola directing an $120m production for a major studio.

Back to that script you've been poring over, and the ticking clock that is already counting down to the start of your Pre-Production Phase.

If you've had the opportunity to read *Decoding The Script* — the first book in this series — you'll have learned how to sift through various Clues the writer has left. Some of those Clues are useful only to the director, while others are helpful and important to everyone else working on the project.

If you haven't read *Decoding* — no harm, no foul. But let me bring you up to speed very quickly and take a moment to remind those who have read *Decoding*, about the essential takeaways from that book.

Decoding The Script discusses two broad types of Clue waiting to be discovered in a well-written and presented script. I call these the 'Primary' Clues and the 'Captain Obvious' Clues.

The 'Primary' Clues deal with aspects of Genre, Theme, Structure, Sub-Text, Texture and Image & Aural Systems. These are Clues that, generally, only Directors fully understand and need. Being able to spot and 'decode' the Primary Six Clues gives Directors the ability to grasp the Form, Structure and underlying meaning of a screenplay and apply their personal focus and 'vision' to shooting, performance and editorial.

The second half of *Decoding The Script* discusses the 'Captain Obvious' Clues. These are the Clues that everyone else involved in the production is particularly concerned about — because they bring up the issues their Department will have to deal with. Issues like 'Cost, Time & Schedule', 'Props, Sets & Picture Vehicles', 'Locations' and 'Casting'.

Alongside the Big Six and the Captain Obvious, *Decoding* also highlights the importance of the First Ten Pages of a screenplay and the 'Special World' being presented. The information given in *Decoding* allows Directors to engage powerfully with the material and have a clear path into Pre-Production. The goal is to have the tools to bring a unique and personal style into Principal Photography and beyond. A signature style that will justify your *'A Film by...'* credit.

Irrespective of whether you have read *Decoding* or not, if the script itself did not give you the necessary Clues to take the script from page to screen, by the time you are through pre-production you will have added elements, ideas and your own 'vision' and interpretation into the mix. You, or a rewrite team, will have worked to make the script 'produce-able' and you will have paid attention to make sure it is 'direct-able'.

For now, let's say that the script satisfied your careful study and has given you an excellent blueprint to begin building the picture. (If you're unsure, you might want to take a peek at *Decoding The Script* to give you some guidance as to where the problems might lie — but enough shameless promotion).

You're the Director, helming this particular vessel, so the Crew will have a myriad of questions to throw at you. Luckily, because 'Captain Obvious' Clues are easy to identify, you'll have spotted where those questions will most likely be, and you'll have some answers ready. Not all the answers, by any means, but enough to start everyone collaborating towards a vision of the film that is *yours*.

Of equal importance, by 'decoding' the Primary Clues, you have information about the making — and *direction* — of this film that nobody else has begun to think about. Yet. You're moving out of development and into pre-production.

Dangerous waters may lie ahead.

- *The choices you make now will directly affect how well your film will perform in the marketplace and, importantly for your future career, how you will be perceived by the industry.*

The demands on your time and energy are about to become enormous. You have to use the 'honeymoon' period in the first phase of Pre-Production to develop your ideas, select what it is you are going to put in front of the camera and plan how you will create entertaining and powerful images from mere words on a page. It's important to use these early stages of Pre-Production, when people are excited about the project, to establish a 'tone' and 'attitude' towards the production that will get everybody working towards the same goal. That goal being... the making of *your* film. In the 'honeymoon' phase, before exhaustion, desperation and disenchantment set in, your collaborators are at their most willing to listen carefully to you and work with your ideas. They want to impress. They want to demonstrate their best work and offer their best ideas. Respect that willingness and don't abuse it. Harness the excitement and energy and use your Pre-Production phase to build a foundation for the project that will withstand the hardships and challenges that lie ahead.

By the end of Pre-Production, you will have gone through a rigorous selection process with every Key Creative involved in Production and Post-Production. If you haven't, if you've skipped or shirked the responsibility, then you only have yourself to blame and you have set yourself up for failure. Pre-Production is a process where you consolidate your team, work out the wrinkles and establish yourself as the guiding creative force. You'll have done this by addressing the majority of the questions, doubts and concerns that have arisen. You will have made the myriad and disparate pieces of your production puzzle into a cohesive and organic whole.

That sounds fine and dandy. But how do you actually do that?

Let us assume — largely because it's both obvious and necessary — that by the time you enter Pre-Production you will have taken the ideas and 'visions' glimpsed during your readings of the screenplay and developed them to the point where you have a clear idea of how you want the screenplay to translate to the screen. You may not know '*how*', but you know the '*why*', the '*where*' and the '*when*'. You have an interpretation of the screenplay that you can discuss and defend. An interpretation that, with the help of your collaborators, can be brought into being. To put it bluntly, you know what you want and how you want it. That knowledge also means that you know what you *don't* want. Your omniscient position of being the lead creator on this project gives you the ability to decide on what is required and what is to be discarded. You are the Great Selector. Your task?

- *Your task is to Select for Success.*

Okay. But how? What are these decisions that are to be made by the Director? What needs to be selected?

Here's The List. There are many responsibilities within these bullet-point categories that others will work to take away from you during pre-production. In fact, that's their job. They want to help by going ahead and getting things done. But even in those areas that don't immediately seem to be the province of the director, you need to stay involved. You must have oversight. You must have awareness. If not, and if things happen without your knowledge or input, then the ship starts to lose direction and the voyage can get very rough indeed. We're going to look at all these 'Departments' and discuss the Director's role in keeping the ship on course.

- Breakdown & Schedule
- Locations
- The Cast
- The Look
- Set Operations
- Production Design
- Stunts & Choreography
- Technical Challenges
- Studios & Sets

- Post Production

There's something vital missing from this List, which I'm sure you will have spotted. That 'something' is;

- The Shot List.

And the reason that it is not included here is twofold.

First, there are filmmakers who are quite happy to make a film without a Shot List. And I have no problem with that. The world of digital filmmaking has freed directors from the shackles of only being able to shoot a limited amount of material. Film negative, in all its flavors from 8mm to 65mm was, and is, expensive. And bulky. Processing the exposed negative in the laboratory was even more expensive. Digital is expensive only in terms of the size of the storage required to hold all the media. There is no longer a requirement to be super-selective about what you shoot, or how much. Point the camera any way you want and keep it running. It's not unusual on film sets nowadays for the camera to remain 'on' after 'cut'. Even the command 'cut' is less frequently used. Producers no longer care about how much you shoot — because there's no cost penalty for them. The penalty now is in the amount of useless material your editor has to sift through — but that's another story.

My second reason for not wishing to discuss the Shot List in this book is because I want to devote an entire volume of *The Filmmaker's Art* series to the subject. Which should indicate that I think building a workable Shot List is important. That's why the next title in this series is *Shooting The List*.

That said, if you don't like working with Shot Lists, then that's your call. You're not alone.

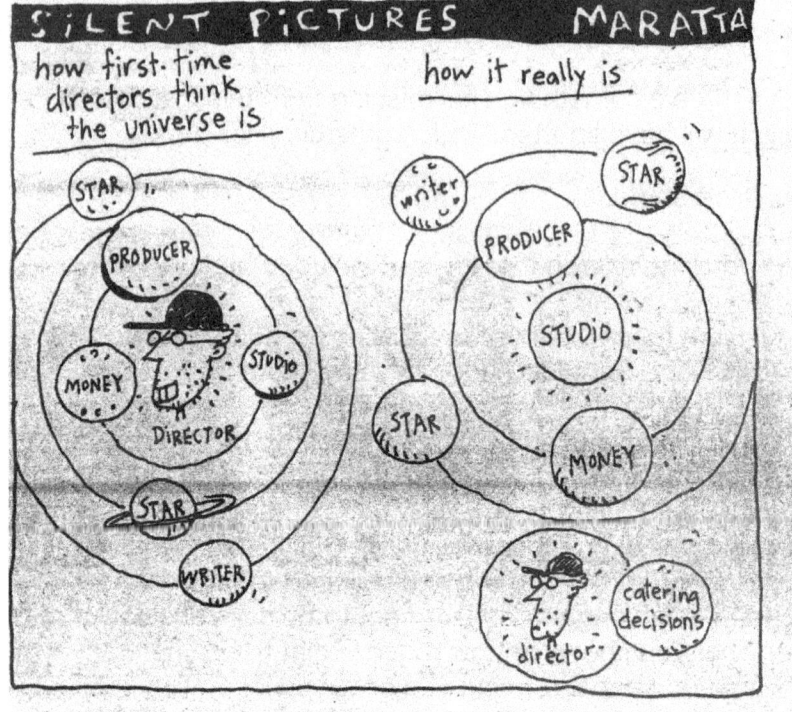

The above cartoon was published in the Los Angeles Times many years ago. Drawn by artist Katie Maratta, (who has graciously allowed me to include it here) 'How First-Time Directors Think The Universe Is', shows two scenarios. First, a youthful and happy film director with planets orbiting around his head, as if he were the center of the Universe. The orbiting planets are variously labeled, 'Star, 'Producer', 'Studio', 'Money' and 'Writer'. Then, alongside the first and entitled, 'How It Really Is', the Director has been replaced at the center of the Universe by 'Studio'. The now unhappy young man has become an outlying planet, entirely detached from the gravitational pull of the Studio. A small, solitary moon orbits around our chastened filmmaker — labelled, 'Catering Decisions'.

Life as a director is not quite the stark reality Katie Maratta's cartoon highlighted, but it's useful to realize that the control you exert, especially in the early stages of your career, is normally dependent on how much the executives decide to give you. My own watchword is; *'No Responsibility Without Authority'*. Be careful that you are not being asked to take responsibility for anything, (including the budget), unless you have the authority to make necessary changes or, at minimum, voice a concern.

Throughout Pre-Production — and depending on the size of your budget, which will naturally affect the size of your production unit — you will meet with all your Department Heads. Line Producer, Unit Production Manager, Assistant Director, Cinematographer/Director of Photography, Production Designer/Art Director, Stunt Coordinator and Key Wardrobe. For some reason, these are the people you most often get to meet, unless there's a specific issue that needs to be addressed — like a meeting with Key Make-Up & Hair. The Production Sound Mixer always seems to be left out — I suspect because nobody understands that sound is important. This means that issues of sound are not yet a priority in anyone's mind. So, we'll be discussing your responsibility in relation to audio in later pages.

The major take-away that this book hopes to give you is the understanding that for every issue that arises — large or small — ultimately, responsibility will be laid at your door. In film production, whenever something is <u>not</u> being accomplished, or even thought about, then it behooves you — the director — to get on top of the situation. And yes, there was real truth in Katie Maratta's joke about what Director's actually control — because with your essential directorial responsibility in mind, you might want to investigate the Catering company and what arrangements are being made for Craft Services. As Napoleon Bonaparte so rightly pointed out; *an army marches on its stomach*. Find out early on what the Producer's attitude to catering is. If it turns out that your Leader thinks paying for crew lunches is an excessive and unwarranted drain on the budget and the plan is to feed everyone for a month on pizza, tuna sandwiches and hamburgers — you have a serious problem.

In the early stages and depending on the demands of the script and your 'vision', you will also meet some or all of your Post-Production Department Heads — Editor, Post-Production Supervisor, Colorist, Visual Effects Supervisor, Supervising Sound Editor, Composer and Music Supervisor. You're going to be taking a lot of meetings and everyone is going to be very polite to you and give you rapt attention. It helps if you have something useful and interesting to say about the project.

Your Department Heads will have read the script and will come to the preliminary meetings with ideas. Some of these ideas and suggestions are brilliant. Others completely misunderstand the point. This is the first moment when you truly direct. Your interpretation of the script must be clear in your mind. If it is not, then the film you make and to which you will attach your name and your future, will merely be a loose amalgamation of everyone else's interpretation. Your job is to unify. To consider and select. To get your team on the same page and going in the same direction. You'll be going through this decision and selection process from now until the film is completed.

Before we go much further in what is going to be a lengthy discussion on 'selection', I feel I should say a word or two about decision-making and its rather ugly cousin, 'compromise'.

You'll be told, or perhaps you already feel, that directors must be decisive. You might have heard, or have come to believe, that to compromise is the ultimate sin. There are those who think (and many of them are film producers) that if you are the type of person who can understand the other person's point-of-view, and who can be swayed by another person's argument — that you are wholly unfit to be, or to become, a director.

Like all dogmas there is an element of truth in this. But it's not the whole truth, or even close to the whole truth. I'll probably repeat it elsewhere, but directors — including the great ones — are often incredibly indecisive and remain so, sometimes after shots have been made and the footage is in the edit. There are even some who remain 'not quite sure' when they're watching the completed film with an audience (although those ultimate moments of dissatisfaction tend to be artistic and creative discontent with one's directorial performance).

To give you an idea of this level of creative indecision, there's a wonderful, but perhaps apocryphal, story of one of the greatest filmmakers of all time — David Lean — making cuts to the print of his latest film (with razor blade and tape) in the back of a taxicab on the way to the world premiere.

Selecting For Success isn't going to attempt to deny your right to creative indecision. The intent is to encourage you to examine, filter, select, and be as decisive as you can be in the moment. But it doesn't mean that you can't change your mind as the camera is being set up, or request something different after a handful of takes are made. It sometimes means that, in pre-production, if you can't decide on the blue or the green — then you ask to have both available on the shoot day. Does the bad guy have that heavy revolver, or the shiny semi-auto? Maybe we wait until we're on set and see how each looks in the actor's hands 'on camera'. Does the blonde wig work on the actress or not? Would it be more effective is she wore the black? They both look great. Does one give more depth to her characterization? Not sure? Can we shoot it both ways? Shall we try her in the red wig?

At the end of this book, there's a slightly sardonic depiction of the type of filmmaker I call "Precious". This filmmaker is very indecisive — but not because he, or she, has come up against a creative 'feeling' that tells them something isn't 'quite right'. Instead, "Precious" has failed to do the work, the preparation, that will help them make a decision, or be able to communicate the reason for their dissatisfaction — and so they lash out with blame and recrimination. The aim of this book is to stop you becoming "Precious".

Again, there's a surly relative of "Precious" who is the kind of filmmaker that refuses 'compromise' because they believe the first duty of a director is *never* to compromise. This type refuses to be grounded in reality. They haven't done any 'selecting for success' by examining the available budget and resources. They haven't considered the multitude of ways that would allow them to realize their 'vision' if only they'd get out of the straitjacket of their blinkered thinking process. No, they want the candy bar, and they want it now — and if they don't get the exact candy bar they've asked for, then they are going to scream, and scream, and scream until they are sick!

- *So, is 'compromise' really the bad thing it's touted to be?*

Well, yeah it is — but only in some respects. If you're compromising because holding out for what you want is too hard, or because you don't want to be seen as difficult, or because you're a people-pleaser and you really don't want to put anyone to any trouble... then, you might be happier in another line of work. To compromise is to accept something that is less than desirable, but filmmaking is full of instances where something 'less than desirable' has to be done. The reasons why are myriad. To name a few; Not enough budget. Not enough time. Not enough available light. The director who stamps his or her foot and screams; "*I will not compromise*", is wasting Time and Energy and starts to look like a fool who should never have been given the job in the first place. The good-to-great director sees the problem, gets quickly up-to-speed on the situation, and then makes a decision that will save the day (or the shot).

The more your filmmaking attracts budgets that can cope with every eventuality, the less you will — as a director — have to find alternative solutions that will keep your 'vision' intact. You need 100 extras for the scene where the marines come storming ashore, in full equipment, guns blazing? You'll get 100. But on a low budget shoot, can you accept 10 extras and still get what you need, without 'compromise'? Well, yes — if you're adept with greenscreen and understand VFX compositing. No matter what your budget, finding alternative ways of doing things and not sticking to the original plan isn't 'directorial compromise'. So, what is meant when people say that Compromise is the great Sin. What is it exactly that directors *lose* if a 'compromise' is made? The answer is simple. They lose the 'vision' they originally had. They lose their *intent*. They lose what would, most likely, have been a 'signature' *moment*

— something in the frame that would define them as a filmmaker.

And that's not good.

Pre-production is the time when you can work to maintain your 'vision', when you can refine that 'vision', when you can see roadblocks to the 'vision' early enough to take an alternative route, or make another choice, that will retain the integrity of your work. Pre-production is where you do the work that prevents 'directorial compromise' — the corruption of your creativity. Pre-production is the phase in the filmmaking process when you are being most closely listened to, so it behooves you to do your work thoroughly and communicate as best as you can. But it's not a phase where you have to arrive at final decisions — although it helps!

In his book *Hope For Film: From The Frontlines of the Independent Cinema Revolutions* (Soft Skull Press), author and producer Ted Hope gives a valuable glimpse into the fine balance that a serious filmmaker must make between indecision and compromise and — importantly — how producers must often give directors space to arrive at a decision, or express discontent, without forcing them into a compromise. Hope tells how, when working with director Ang Lee, he began to understand his director's decision-making process. He learned to ask the director the questions that would help bring about a final decision. Ang Lee would not compromise — but the only way to tell that he wasn't fully satisfied was by his quiet demeanor and a rather shy and anxious expression. Even when pressed, Ang Lee would respond that he was 'okay' with whatever it was that clearly bothered him. Hope and the crew would realize that 'okay' meant that Ang was not 'okay' — judging this from tone of voice, facial expression and previous experience. So, they'd ask questions that would elicit the responses which would tell them what the director was thinking. With that information they were then able to fully realize the director's 'vision'.

An outside observer might look at that kind of scenario and think; *'Why has this guy been made the director — he can't come to a decision, and if he's unable to say what's wrong then surely he's going to compromise his 'vision' by default?*

But the scenario is much, much more common than you would imagine. Directors need to think. It's not unusual for the director to be standing by the camera pondering, a gloomy look on their face. There will sometimes be some communication — a cinematographer breaking the silence by making a suggestion. Crews who have worked with the director before, totally 'get' it. The crew understand the problem, or at least are aware that something isn't fitting the director's 'vision'. They're prepared to wait for their director — and leap into action when the command decision comes down.

Incidentally, some directors will allow a crew member at the sharp end of the problem — a Key Grip, for example — to chime in and suggest a solution or ask what they could do to help retain the 'vision'. It's not a sign of weakness when a director solicits opinions from the crew, it's actually helping others to 'own' their work on the film and engenders a positive team spirit. One aspect of good leadership is the ability to let others bring their best ideas, and to instill focus and determination within the group. Robert Altman, it is said, believed in collaboration so completely that he would accept a suggestion from literally anybody on his crew — including lowly production assistants — knowing that if the suggestion created a brilliant solution that he hadn't thought of, the credit would still read 'A Film by Robert Altman'

Sometimes, after these ponderings, and discussions with the crew, a director will seem (to an outsider) to "compromise" — by doing the shot in a different way or abandoning an idea completely. But, that's not 'directorial compromise' — that's directing.

With luck and good judgment, you will hook up with a savvy Producer who sees it as her task to give you, within reason, everything you need to get the job done right. More important still, she will understand when you have reached a moment of indecision and be able to coax out of you the response that is going to help both her, and the crew, give you what you're reaching for. That Producer will work with you as a partner — listening to your 'vision' and, more important still, trusting you to take the project to a place she has only dreamed about.

This is why you were attached to the project in the first place — to use your unique 'vision', your skills, your personality and, yes, sometimes your connections within the industry, to make the project come to life in ways that others couldn't.

However, there will come times when decisions — and some selections — are taken out of your control. I'll discuss the more common of these as we proceed. For now, let's imagine that the production is blank — waiting for you to call it into being.

CHAPTER TWO

Breakdown & Schedule

One of the most significant problems you will ever face as a Director is the management of Time. Time is the Enemy. Time is not your Friend. On a movie production Time is extremely limited. Even directors working with multi-million-dollar budgets on shoots that span 120 days or more of Principal Photography feel the pressure of Time.

Lines from a metaphysical poem written by Andrew Marvell in the 1650's, seem to have been crafted with Directors in mind;

But at my back I always hear,
Time's winged chariot hurrying near.

Except, in our case, Time's winged chariot is a producer tapping his watch and wondering if we really need the next shot.

The Management of Time becomes vital for successful 'on budget' film production. Everything to do with the production — from the 'call-times' for crew and cast to arrive on set, to the equipment needed for a particular day, for the number of extras required in a scene or the specific days an actor or location or vital element is available — all that has to be managed in terms of Time and slotted into a scheduled plan.

The plan I'm talking about boils down to two basic documents. A Script Breakdown and a Production Schedule. Depending on the size of the production, a Breakdown & Schedule will be prepared by either the Producer, Line Producer, Unit Production Manager (UPM) or First Assistant Director (1st A.D). Or you, the Director. Or a combination of two or more of the above.

It's possible, although unlikely, to make a movie without a Script Breakdown or a Production Schedule. But because Time is paramount, and because everybody needs to know what is required for each scene, these two documents are of vital importance.

To 'breakdown' the script into its relevant parts is relatively simple, a data-input task easily done with a variety of available production management software. Entertainment Partners' *Movie Magic* is gold-standard, (E.P. also offers the newer and clunkily-named *Scenechronize* which is a full production office project management tool). *StudioBinder* is a very useful online app and is free for a single project. Many folk turn to Jungle Software's *Gorilla*, and some are using *Celtx*. If you're old school, you could download and print a Breakdown Sheet template and fill everything in with pen and pencil — which saves tears if your computer is prone to crashing.

The Breakdown is as it sounds. Each scene is broken down into its separate elements. Location. Exterior or Interior. Night or Day. Number of Pages. Cast. Extras. Vehicles. Props. Stunts. Special Effects. Special Equipment. Animals. Your job is to check the Breakdown against the script — and your own needs. The writer won't have indicated in the script how to 'direct' the scene visually — that's your department — but if your 'vision' calls for a crane shot, or a Steadicam™, or a particular lens or lighting effect, then it needs to be in the Breakdown because the Breakdown is going to go to your Department Heads and become their most important reference. You also need to check that nothing is missing or has been miscalculated. If the Line Producer has entered 6 extras for a scene that you feel needs 60 then a conversation is past due. The Breakdown is your movie's Bible, and you are 'God', so make sure everything is in there. Make sure it's updated if things get changed, eliminated or added.

But let's imagine that there is no Breakdown. Your Producer is too busy, and the U.P.M. or A.D. aren't on board yet. Like so many things in film production, it really helps if you know how to accomplish the task yourself.

On the next page is an example for us to work with. Two brief scenes, a single page, from an unproduced screenplay — *Cedric's Long Walk*. These two scenes are part of a sequence featuring a homeless man and a lost child.

When a Schedule is being prepared, the first step is to allocate each scene its own Breakdown Sheet. Data entry is started by entering the information the script gives in the 'Slugline'. In our example, we would have two separate Breakdown pages, one for Sc. 64 and another for Sc 65.

Scene 64 is a NIGHT EXTERIOR on a Wasteground location with the two principal characters (HARRY HIPPIE and CEDRIC) and the added element of RAIN.

Scene 65 is I/E — a scene that is both INTERIOR *and* EXTERIOR— given that the action requires players to move through an open doorway. The RAIN from Sc. 64 is still present, and the two principals have been joined by a group of costumed EXTRAS (Bedraggled Men) and a supporting player (STAFFER). The location, as written, is an actual Los Angeles shelter for the homeless, but a substitute is likely to be used.

WHITE Revision - 5-1-07   40.

64   EXT. WASTEGROUND -- NIGHT   64

     RAINING hard as **HARRY** leads **CEDRIC** back to his home. Harry
     shakes his fist at the rain. He begins to cover up his
     shopping cart - and Cedric helps him. Harry grunts his
     thanks. He grabs an overstuffed plastic bag and heads off.

                         HARRY HIPPIE
                   C'mon, Jug!

65   I/E. MIDNIGHT MISSION -- NIGHT   65

     RAINING hard. **BEDRAGGLED MEN** cluster around the doorway,
     waiting to get in. **HARRY** and **CEDRIC** amongst them.

     THE ADMISSION COUNTER -- HARRY and CEDRIC watch as the MEN
     in front of them check with the **STAFFER** and go through the
     turnstile. Then it's Harry's turn.

                         STAFFER
                   Sign in, Harry.

     Harry takes the clipboard and starts to write laboriously.

                         STAFFER (CONT'D)
                     (noticing Cedric)
                   Wait a minute...who's this?

     Harry looks up, totally innocent.

                         STAFFER (CONT'D)
                   Harry, what's this kid doing here?

                         HARRY HIPPIE
                   That's only Jug, he's alright.

                         CEDRIC
                     (shouts to Staffer)
                   No! My name's Cedric Hawkins. And
                   he won't let me go!

     The Staffer takes one more look at the pair and reaches for
     the phone. As he dials...

                         STAFFER
                   Harry, don't you move! You stay
                   right there!

     Harry, in panic, pushes past the MEN. Pulling Cedric along.

                         STAFFER (CONT'D)
                   Harry! Come back here!

                         CEDRIC (O.S.)
                   He won't let me go!!

                                          Filmworks, U.S.A. L.L.C.

All these elements will make it into their respective Breakdown Sheets, along with; specific props (such as the SHOPPING CART and OVERSTUFFED BAG in Sc. 64 and the Staffer's CLIPBOARD, PEN and PHONE for Sc. 65). Specialized equipment may be included (such as additional lighting for night shooting, or camera support tools that the Director and Cinematographer have agreed on). The number of EXTRAS required to be 'Bedraggled Men' will be indicated, along with any specific costuming, make-up or wigs for the characters. The TURNSTILE mentioned in Sc. 65 might be noted under Set Dressing if it is not part of a physical location.

If you look at the image that follows — a completed Breakdown Sheet for our Sc. 65 example, — you'll see that it includes everything mentioned in the script and several items that are not. This is an important point. A Breakdown will include many items that are *not* found in the script — but which are the result of both the Director's 'vision' and the team's requirements following the 'tech recce' or 'scout' of the locations to be used.

What has happened is that the Director (in this case, yours truly) has had a look at the script and the proposed locations and has then gone beyond the writer's plain narrative to get more bang out of the scene, both visually and in terms of action. Given his interpretive 'vision', the Director has met with the relevant Department Heads and the Producer and put forward his concepts. These have been green-lit and the budget adjusted. Usually there's a trade-off and smart Directors will *give* in order to *get* — but more on that later.

Scene # 65 Script Page: 40 Page Count: 6/8 pgs.	**BREAKDOWN SHEET** Cedric's Long Walk	Date: 8/19/2018 Sheet: 65 Int/Ext: INT/EXT Day/Night: NIGHT

Scene Description: Harry attempts to sign in
Setting: MIDNIGHT MISSION
Location: TBD
Sequence: HARRY HIPPE   Script Day: _____

Page 1

Cast Members 8. CEDRIC 29. HARRY 58. STAFFER	VEHICLES: PATROL CAR DRIVE-BY STUNT CAR FOR PRECISION STOP	STUNTS: HARRY PUSH THRU BACKGROUND ARTISTS (— POSSIBLE FALL) (W/ TABLE COLLAPSE) PRECISION DRIVER — HARD STOP
EXTRAS/ATMOS: BEDRAGGLED MEN (6)	LIGHTING/GRIP ADDL: 12KW FRENEL HMI TOW GENERATOR 800a 60' CONDOR 16' JIMMY JIB or SIMILAR w/ HOTHEAD	MUAH: PREP FOR RAIN (TOWELS, HAIRDRYERS) ADD ASSISTANT FOR BACKGROUND PERFORMERS
CAMERA: RAIN COVER	PROPS: PHONE CLIPBOARD PEN OVERSTUFFED BAG LEASH & COLLAR	COSTUME/WARDROBE: CEDRIC x 4 HARRY x 4 PREP FOR RAIN
SPECIAL EQUIPMENT: RAINMAKER — WATER TRUCK	SET DRESSING: TURNSTILE (POSSIBLE BREAKAWAY TABLE FOR STUNT)	STUDIO TEACHER: YES

DIRECTOR'S NOTES: CRANE SHOT FROM HI-ANGLE TO DOORWAY & REVERSE TO BOOKEND SCENE

PRODUCTION NOTES: TRAFFIC CONTROL FOR ALL EXTERIOR SHOTS. 2ND MEAL FOR LATE WRAP.

In this example, a STUNT has been added, because the Director felt the scene deserved more than Harry merely 'pushing through the men' as the script would have it. One or more of the Background Performers are going to be bowled over — probably just one, given the differential between the Day Rate for a Stunt Player and a Background Artist. What's more, there's a table or some other furniture, chairs maybe, that are going to be broken or knocked over when the bedraggled Stunt Player makes his fall. So, you'll notice 'POSSIBLE BREAKAWAY TABLE' in the Set Dressing box.

Under Director's Notes, a CRANE SHOT is mentioned — to 'bookend' the scene. In other words, the crane will be used for shots to open and close the scene. The Director has a HI-ANGLE shot in mind for the scene's opening that will crane down, and over, the Bedraggled Men huddled outside the shelter. (Crane shots always look amazing in rain.) Then, for the scene's closing shot, the Crane will lift into a WIDE Shot to see Harry run off across the street, dragging Cedric with him (an action that is not mentioned in the script).

If you look at the Stunts and Vehicles categories, you'll notice a precision-driven 'HARD STOP' — which is a car braking hard in the rain, as Harry and Cedric dash into the street. The Production Notes are all over this with their TRAFFIC CONTROL.

Production has also noted that because it's a night shoot, using artificial RAIN, and with a child as part of a couple of stunts — the crew might be going home late, and a 2nd MEAL has been allowed for. Because of the child actor, it has also been noted that a STUDIO TEACHER will be present. Make-Up & Hair (MUAH) has been reminded to bring TOWELS and HAIR-DRYERS because there's going to be a lot of wet actors. Wardrobe has been put on notice that they will need FOUR changes of costume for the principals. Lighting & Grip know they will have an additional light(s) for the night shoot, along with a TOW GENERATOR (which alerts the production office for permits and parking). A CONDOR (a boom lift platform) has been added with a 60' rise — which will take the 12kw HMI high enough to light a wide area and stay out of shot. And a crane or JIB with a remote HOT-HEAD has been added to the breakdown for those opening and closing shots. An LAPD PATROL CAR, not mentioned in the script, is listed in Vehicles. In the actual script, the patrol car is not required until Sc 66, but by adding it to Sc 65 the director is getting full value out of the rental, and will probably have it drive-by, perhaps at speed with light bars flashing, as the Crane begins its downward movement at the start of the scene. Finally, there's an issue of continuity — revealed by the addition of 'LEASH & COLLAR' under props. Harry, you see, is mentally ill and has confused Cedric with his lost dog, 'Jug'. He's been towing Cedric around on Jug's collar and leash — and so props that were part of previous scenes have to be noted in Sc. 64 & 65 too — or somebody will be able to shrug and say *'It wasn't in the Breakdown'* if the items don't make it onto set.

I think you can see that this Breakdown adds some visual and action elements that are not present in the screenplay. The point I'm making is that left to their own devices, 1st A.D.s, U.P.M.s and Line Producers can get very literal. If it's in the script, it goes in the Breakdown. If it's not in the script, it's not planned for. Only as a result of meetings with Cinematographers, Production Designers, Stunt Coordinators and the Production Office does the Breakdown start to get fully filled out — but it is almost entirely dependent on the Director having a 'vision' for the scene that is properly communicated. It's no use turning up on the night of the shoot and saying; *'I think I'd like to start with a crane shot over the Extras, with the patrol car going by'* if nobody has been told earlier that's what you want. There will be no crane and no patrol car. Your 1st A.D., U.P.M., and Line Producer will shrug. Your 'vision' is now *kaput*. No use blaming anyone other than yourself. (And yes, there are Directors who come onto set unprepared, ask for something that hasn't been planned for, have a hissy fit and send everyone scrambling for the 'missing' elements. You don't want to be one of those).

Anything still missing from Sc. 65? Or wrong? Well, will 6 Bedraggled Men be enough? I don't think so! My shot needs 15! Will the producer give me another 9 Extras and adjust the budget accordingly? If so, then the cost of Background Performers is going to increase. Does that mean I'll have to give up around $1,125 of value that has already been allocated elsewhere? Probably!

'Selecting For Success' means that your task is to either enter data yourself or check that the Breakdown Sheet has everything required. Here's a vital tip. Pay particular attention that DAY and NIGHT and INT and EXT have been transferred correctly to the Sheet. There is nothing worse than planning a shoot day for Daylight Interior scenes, only to discover that an error crept into the Breakdown (and subsequently the Stripboard) and an important sunlit interior scene that should have been put into the schedule for that day has been labelled Night Exterior and added to a night shoot three days hence.

A minor point. When you build a Breakdown, each character is assigned an identification number. Characters in principal roles get the first numbers (and usually the 'Big Star' will be assigned #1). Lesser roles will have later numbers — #22, #34 etc. The Breakdown Sheet will indicate both the character ID# and the character name. That ID number transfers into the Stripboard, sometimes making it difficult to see at a glance who is in the scene — but scheduling software will sometimes give you an option to use character names instead.

Last, but far from least. Each Breakdown sheet has an almost unnoticed piece of data of great significance. Film Production, you will recall, is all about Time Management. Clearly, before we begin to put a Schedule together, we have to have some idea of how long it will take to shoot each scene. For this reason, the Breakdown Sheet includes a 'Page Count' for the scene.

That's the 'why' — here's the 'how'.

For a Production Breakdown, script pages are broken down into 1/8ths. A full page in a correctly-formatted screenplay is 8/8ths. Half a page is 4/8ths. A three-line paragraph might be 1/8th of a page. Six lines usually adds up to 2/8ths of a page. It doesn't have to be exact — but it does have to be close. A scene that runs for three full pages and for a small portion of a fourth page, might then be entered as 3 and 3/8ths pages. In the script example we've been using, you'll see that Sc 64 is about 2/8ths of a page, and the rest of the page is 6/8ths.

Before we head into explaining this Time Management aspect of Scheduling, and the resulting Stripboard, allow me to quickly familiarize you with Computerized Data Entry using proprietary Scheduling Software.

The example that follows is a cropped image of the data entry window of the Breakdown Sheet for Scene 65 created in a version of Jungle Software's *Gorilla* application. The header for Sc. 65 shows a Shoot Day date — meaning the scene has been auto-scheduled for that day. That might change once we are deeper in Scheduling, in which case we over-ride the computer's calculation and put the human touch into our Scheduling.

For now, notice that the upper third of the Breakdown sheet opposite includes the Slug-line data. We can see at a glance that we're dealing with Sc. 65 at the Midnight Mission location. A brief synopsis reminds everyone of the scene's main purpose. Then, on the top right, we find the all-important Night or Day, and underneath the D/N box is the equally important Page Count, which here is 6/8ths of a page. The Breakdown Sheet has a specific number (which in this case is the same as the Scene number), and we're also given the actual Script Page this Breakdown Sheet relates to.

SELECTING FOR SUCCESS | 35

Day Number: 12				Shoot Day: Sun., Aug. 19, 2018			
I/E	INT/EXT	Set	MIDNIGHT MISSION			D/N	NIGHT
Scene #s	65					Pages	6 /8
Synopsis	Harry attempts to sign in					Sheet #	65
Location						End of Day	8/19/2018
Prod. Phase	Principal Photography		Sequence		Script Day	Script Page	40

Categories	Show: ALL Cast Members	All Elements for this Breakdown Sheet	
Cast Members (66)	ASIAN COOK (1)	BEDRAGGLED MEN	Extras
Extras (142)	BEAUTIFUL WOMAN (2)	8. CEDRIC	Cast Members
Stunts (14)	BEVERLY (3)	CLIPBOARD	Props
Vehicles (42)	BIG MAN (4)	COLLAR	Props
Props (216)	BOBBY (5)	29. HARRY	Cast Members
Special Effects (0)	BONE (6)	LEASH	Props
Costumes (14)	BONES (7)	OVERSTUFFED BAG	Props
Makeup (4)	CEDRIC (8)	PEN	Props
Livestock (0)	CHARLIE (9)	PHONE	Props
Animal Handler (4)	CLERK (10)	PHONE	Props
Music (0)	CONCHA (11)	RAIN	Special
Sound (0)	COOK (12)	58. STAFFER	Cast Members
Set Dressing (41)	COP (13)	TURNSTILE	Set Dressing

Because the above diagram is the data entry window of a computer-generated Breakdown, it confusingly shows three columns. In this application, the Left column navigates to Categories, the center shows all the Elements in a selected category *for the entire project*, while the third column to the far right shows the Elements selected for the specific scene. You'll notice our example includes Cast, Extras, Props, Special Equipment and Set Dressing. Clicking on an Element brings it into the Breakdown for that scene— a quick and accurate process.

Is it worthwhile using computer programs rather than the old-fashioned paper and pencil? Yes, of course. Not least because you can 'tag' the screenplay so that all the required elements *within the script* can be imported into the Breakdown in a matter of seconds. However, you still have to make sure that everything you require to *direct* the scene has been included and those new Elements will have to be entered manually. Sometimes, you can wait until whoever is doing the data entry has printed out the Breakdown Sheets — and then add your requirements by hand — with the resulting Breakdown then being scanned, copied or data re-entered. Or you take over the computer yourself and add the new elements following your discussions with Department Heads and Production Office. The Breakdown is quite organic, you see. It's built by many hands — but you have to have oversight.

With a complete Breakdown of the entire script and of every scene that you are going to shoot during Principal Photography, you now have your Production Bible — a weighty document (whether as a file or hard copy) that can be distributed amongst your Key Department Heads so they can go to work with a complete reference for the entire shoot. This is the primary purpose of the Breakdown. The secondary purpose is equally important — the Breakdown provides the information required to construct your Production Schedule, a document more familiarly known as The Stripboard.

For clarity, let me remind you that films are seldom shot 'in continuity'. There are exceptions, such as; (i) the 'single shot' film (*Russian Ark*, 2002), (ii) the film that is essentially a filmed stage-play (*Rope,* 1948), (iii) the film that exists in a single (or limited number of) space(s) in a linear time frame (*The Bitter Tears of Petra Von Kant*,1972). However, the majority of films have multiple locations, multiple 'times of day', multiple actors that pop in and out of the 'continuous' timeline, scenes that occur before the main action begins, or long after. It's a jumble and it could be a mess.

The Stripboard organizes that mess.

How do we bring order out of chaos? First, we sort according to broad parameters. Scenes that will be shot on Sound Stages are grouped separately from those that will be shot on Location. Locations will be grouped according to the distance between them and the days that they will be available. Scenes in one location will grouped together, and then further sub-grouped into Morning/Day/Dusk/Night. This basic sorting may sound easy enough — but then there are issues of Actor Availability that will poke holes in your careful plan. There are also issues of readiness (where days are needed to prepare a stage set or location). That leads to issues of 'company moves' — perhaps a few miles, perhaps a few hundred miles, perhaps a different continent. Then there are the issues of key crew, facility or equipment availability (the Stunt Coordinator currently in Hong Kong, the Stage that is booked during your first week of filming, the special lens that you can have only on a Tuesday). The variables are vast. Too vast for your $300 app, but solvable by the human brain, once engaged.

In olden times, we would use our IBM electric 'golf ball' typewriters to complete our blank pre-printed Breakdown Sheets, and then — by hand and pen — we'd export the data found in the Breakdown to the Schedule by writing each Scene's information onto colored card strips — strips about 12" to 15" long and 1/4" wide. Starting with the all-important Scene Number, INTERIOR DAY scenes would be written on WHITE strips and EXTERIOR DAY would be YELLOW. INTERIOR NIGHT would get a BLUE strip, and EXTERIOR NIGHT would be GREEN. Once all the scenes for a specific day had been entered, we'd separate each shoot day with a BLACK strip. This convention has been carried through to scheduling software, with some minor modifications. Because writing apps have given screenwriters the ability to have Morning, Dawn, Twilight and Dusk options rather than just DAY and NIGHT, many scheduling apps have added PINK for DAWN EXTERIOR, ORANGE for DUSK EXTERIOR and GREY for EVENING EXTERIOR along with various other colors for DAY OFF, TRAVEL DAY, etc.

In addition to the INT/EXT/, DAY/NIGHT and Scene Number Heading, each strip would include; (i) a number indicating which Breakdown Sheet it was related to, (ii) how many pages were in the Scene, (iii) a brief synopsis and, crucially, (iv) the ID number or Character Name which related to each cast member present in the scene.

- Scene Number
- Interior or Exterior

- Time of Day
- Location
- Synopsis
- How Many Pages
- Cast

Once all the information had been entered, we'd end up with a colorful bunch of around 100 to 200 strips — depending on how many scenes were in the script.

Then came the hard part. The strips were inserted into a Board (The Stripboard) in the sequence that we intended to shoot. Now, of course, computers will do the heavy lifting. Your computer-generated Breakdown is imported into The (Virtual) Stripboard and scenes can then be organized into the agreed order for shooting.

I know you're asking yourself what all this has to do with 'Directing'. After all, these are details that could, and should, be handled by persons in the Production Office. You'll find me repeating myself, but the answer is always the same. You need to know how things are done, in case there is a failure on someone else's part — but, more importantly (especially at the budget-conscious, minimally-experienced end of film production), people who are not given the responsibility of directing often don't care how achievable their scheduling is. Let me illuminate.

In today's dollars, my first theatrical feature had a budget of $1.8m. Not chump change. Enough of a budget to hire experienced film professionals in all departments. Back then, I barely understood feature film scheduling and left it to those professionals. The first day of shooting turned out to involve three 'company moves' within a busy urban environment on a foreign location, often using a process trailer (low loader) to shoot dialogue scenes with actors in a car. Each move to the next location took a good 90 minutes. The final scenes were in a harbor. These involved 'gunfire', window shatter effects, blood sprays, special FX make-up, police vehicles with multiple costumed Extras, and a complicated crane shot. I went 'over' on Day One by about 2.5 hours. The Daily Report put the Completion Bond company on notice that the first-time director had encountered difficulty in 'making the day' — and they started planning to replace me if I didn't speed up and 'make the week'. The Producer noted that the extra 2.5 hours had eaten up some of his budget and started to plan where he would make the necessary savings and adjustments. In other words, he started planning how to cut scenes. The Assistant Director realized that he'd have to push the crew harder and, thinking that the Director was not up to the task, shared his fears with the Production Office. But I understood that my fault wasn't in being slow, it was in trusting that the Schedule was viable. I knew my crane shot would take a lot of time to execute. I knew that using a process trailer always eats time. I should have investigated the distance and time involved in crossing the city. If I'd thought about it more carefully, and not assumed that someone in the Production Office knew what they were doing, I would have realized that the Schedule was too ambitious for me. I should have axed one of the 'moves' so I'd get to the harbor earlier and then picked up the dropped scenes on another day. I didn't — but, boy, did I learn. That's why knowledge of Scheduling is important for you. You have to bring to it an awareness of what you can do in the available time and what you can't do and be able to spot when you are being set up for failure however inadvertently it happens, or however well-meaning the overly-optimistic are. So, let's get to it.

    In the spirit of keeping it simple, let's imagine that it had already been decided that Principal Photography will span 4 weeks, with 1 day off each week. Yes, we're in 'low budget' world. 4 weeks of 6-day weeks will give us a 24-day shooting schedule. We turn to the back of our screenplay example, *Cedric's Long Walk,* where the last page is revealed to be #108. How convenient! Simple math will inform us how many pages of the script need to be shot each day to make that 24-day Schedule. In this case, 4 pages per day.

This is why we needed a Page Count for each Scene entered into the Breakdown Sheet and then imported into the, as yet, unsorted Schedule. We can now make a further sub-division in our sorting — and try to schedule each day to be as close to 4 pages as possible.

Now, scheduling apps can do this sorting automatically, and production office staff can also take a stab at it — but the truth is, unless the A.D., and/or U.P.M., are really experienced and know how you work, the likelihood of either the computer or the Production Office getting it right is slim. If your production allocates 10 shooting hours per day, and the schedule demands a four-page day then — on *Cedric's Long Walk* — for every 2.5 hours that passes, you need to have shot a full page of the script to keep on schedule. 8/8ths every 2.5 hours. The computer only sees 'page eighths'. It has no idea how long that 'eighth' will take to shoot. Experienced A.D.s/U.P.M.s have a better idea of the problems. They know that sometimes an 'eighth' of a page might take all day to shoot, while in half-a-day it's possible to shoot 7 pages of dialogue.

Let's go back and consider Sc. 64 and 65. Night. Rain. Big and tricky lighting. Two different locations, which we'll assume are fairly close to each other. A stunt fall, and a precision driving stunt in one of the scenes. A child actor who, in Los Angeles, can work only 8 hours on a non-school day. If we were shooting in New Jersey (which we're not, but if we were), young 'Cedric' could only be 'on set' for five hours.

You go back to the Stripboard. Sc. 64 is 2/8ths of a page. You could probably get the whole scene in 3 shots. Maybe just one. But the set-up is intense. If you want to avoid it being static, you're setting up a motion shot — probably a dolly on track unless you have a good camera stabilizer and you can walk the movement over rough ground. But you could easily eat up 2 hours on this scene. Almost as much time as math and the Schedule tells us you'd have to shoot a full page, not a mere 2/8ths. Sc. 65, at 6/8ths gives you a 'full page', but with Sc. 64 eating up almost 2 hours, the 'on paper' requirement is to finish off Sc. 65 in 30 minutes. Trying to remain 'in continuity' and go from Sc. 64 to 65 — which, let's imagine, includes a 'company move' that will eat up much of that remaining 30 minutes — doesn't look like the brightest idea. Sc. 65 has the Crane, the Patrol Car, wet Extras, a Stunt Performer, an HMI that needs to go up on the Condor, difficulties in keeping the camera dry and rigging the Crane. How long to shoot this dialogue/action scene? 3 hours? Add in Sc 64, and a minor 'company move', and we're knocking on six hours to get a *single* page of the screenplay shot. We are short 3 pages and only four hours left in our 10-hour day. A solution? Sure. There's probably a 3-page sequence (mostly dialogue, you hope) that could fill up the remaining 4 hours of your day. But you'd want to shoot it first so that (i) you can move to the night shoot knowing you've already shot 75% of your 'day' and (ii) an advance crew can start to set up the Wasteground and the Homeless Shelter to maximize efficiency. What's the big danger? Time, of course. But let's say you shoot that early 3-page scene and it takes the estimated 4 hours. You're feeling golden, because you think you're right on schedule. Darkness falls, and you go to the Shelter or the Wasteground locations. Everything's cool, right? Wrong. The child actor has only got 4 hours left. If you're on the Wasteground and it takes 2.5 hours to get the scene, you now have to do the far more complex Sc. 65 in 90 minutes, or you lose the child. Solution? There's always a solution. You go to the Wasteground *after* the Shelter. Sc. 64 is not as important as Sc. 65. If you manage to make it, then great. You'll most likely give Sc. 64 a try in any case, even if it means going over by 30 minutes (and you could argue that the 'company move' meant the child was not 'on set' — so 'Cedric' won't get whisked away.)

I apologize for dragging you through these convoluted mock scenarios, but it's important that you see how much you need to keep tabs on the Stripboard. In film production, there are variables involved that only you — and excellent A.D.s, Producers and U.P.M.s — are sensitive to.

In our example of a 4-pages per day schedule, a 3 and 3/8ths page scene might take most of a day to shoot — but still require us to shoot a further 5/8ths of a page to 'make the day'. The trick in Scheduling is to find that additional 5/8ths of a page in, ideally, the same Location, in the same 'Time' (Day/Night) and with the same, or available, Cast. Perhaps we get lucky and find a short scene that is 2/8ths and another that is 4/8ths. A total of 6/8ths. We were hoping for 5/8ths — but we'll take the extra 1/8th and put those three scenes into the Schedule for a single complete day of 4 and 1/8th pages.

Gradually, the Stripboard will take shape. Problems will emerge — mostly to do with trying to keep Locations, 'Time of Day' and Available Cast in a good consecutive order. But we'll keep re-arranging the strips until we have it in as satisfactory a shooting sequence as possible.

The next image shows a section from a computer-generated Stripboard. Unfortunately, within the print version of this book (and some e-book versions), you'll only see it in black and white — but in the back you'll find a link to my site where you can download a free and full-color version not only of a Stripboard but also sample pages of a Breakdown and a Production Budget. (These free downloads are available on the Media page of my website — markusinnocenti.com).

The sample Stripboard that follows is a mix of Yellow (Ext/Day), White (Int/Day), Grey (Ext/Evening) and Green (Ext/Night) strips, showing the schedule for Days 10 thru 13 in the *Cedric's Long Walk* production. Please take a look at the total Pages scheduled to be shot each day — found in the black 'End of Day' strip. Not all days manage to hit the magic 4-page/day mark we require to complete this shoot on time and on budget — so the Schedule will need to compensate somewhere.

Sheet: 109	Scenes: 109	EXT NEAR THE TOWERS, WATTS Cedric meets Deon	DAY	0 4/8 pgs.	CEDRIC, DEON
Sheet: 111	Scenes: 111	EXT RAILROAD TRACKS, WATTS Deon and Cedric play a dangerous game	DAY	1 0/8 pgs.	CEDRIC, DEON
Sheet: 110	Scenes: 110	INT KITCHEN/DEON'S HOME, WATTS Deon's Mom cleans Cedric's wound	DAY	1 0/8 pgs.	CEDRIC, DEON, DEON'S MOM, DEON'S MOM
Sheet: 112	Scenes: 112	EXT DEON'S HOME, WATTS Cedric can't sleep over with Deon	EVENING	0 6/8 pgs.	CEDRIC, DEON, DEON'S MOM, DEON'S MOM
		-- END OF DAY 10 -- Friday, August 17, 2018		3 3/8 pgs.	
Sheet: 45	Scenes: 45	EXT TENEMENT BUILDING Ulmer and Fuller climb the stairs	DAY	1 2/8 pgs.	DETECTIVE FULLER, DETECTIVE ULMER, FULLER, ULMER
Sheet: 46	Scenes: 46	INT ROLANDA'S APARTMENT -- MOMENTS LATER Ulmer and Fuller check the apartment	DAY	0 3/8 pgs.	DETECTIVE FULLER, DETECTIVE ULMER, FULLER, ULMER
Sheet: 58	Scenes: 58	EXT GAS STATION Harry grabs Cedric	NIGHT	0 6/8 pgs.	CEDRIC, HARRY, HARRY HIPPIE
Sheet: 63	Scenes: 63	EXT NEAR TENT CITY Heading back, it starts to rain	NIGHT	0 1/8 pgs.	CEDRIC, HARRY
Sheet: 59	Scenes: 59	EXT WASTEGROUND Harry believes that Cedric is his dog	NIGHT	1 2/8 pgs.	CEDRIC, HARRY, HARRY HIPPIE
Sheet: 64	Scenes: 64	EXT WASTEGROUND The rain comes down hard	NIGHT	0 2/8 pgs.	CEDRIC, HARRY, HARRY HIPPIE
		-- END OF DAY 11 -- Saturday, August 18, 2018		4 pgs.	
Sheet: 53	Scenes: 53	EXT TENT CITY, SAN PEDRO STREET Cedric runs through the homeless	DAY	0 2/8 pgs.	CEDRIC
Sheet: 51	Scenes: 51	EXT 4TH STREET GARMENT DISTRICT Cedric near the Midnight Mission	DAY	0 1/8 pgs.	CEDRIC
Sheet: 65	Scenes: 65	INT/EXT MIDNIGHT MISSION Harry attempts to sign in	NIGHT	6/8 pgs.	CEDRIC, HARRY, HARRY HIPPIE, STAFFER, STAFFER
Sheet: 66	Scenes: 66	EXT ALLEY, NEAR MIDNIGHT MISSION Cops question Harry	NIGHT	1 2/8 pgs.	CEDRIC, HARRY, HARRY HIPPIE, OFFICER IN RAIN, OFFICER IN RAIN
Sheet: 67	Scenes: 67	EXT INNER CITY STREETS Cedric runs for his life	NIGHT	0 3/8 pgs.	CEDRIC
		-- END OF DAY 12 -- Sunday, August 19, 2018		2 6/8 pgs.	
Sheet: 85	Scenes: 85	INT LOW RENT UNIT, SPANISH CRENSHAW The girls decide to give Cedric a bath	DAY	1 3/8 pgs.	CEDRIC, CONCHA, NESSA, NESSA, OFELIA, OFELIA, SANDRA, SANDRA
Sheet: 86	Scenes: 86	INT BATHROOM, LOW RENT UNIT Cedric takes a bath	DAY	0 7/8 pgs.	CEDRIC, NESSA, NESSA, OFELIA, OFELIA, SANDRA, SANDRA
Sheet: 87	Scenes: 87	INT BEDROOM, LOW RENT UNIT The girls want to know about Cedric's family	DAY	1 3/8 pgs.	CEDRIC, CONCHA, NESSA, NESSA, OFELIA, OFELIA, SANDRA, SANDRA
Sheet: 88	Scenes: 88	INT KITCHEN, LOW RENT UNIT The girls try to reach Robert Hawkins	DAY	0 7/8 pgs.	CEDRIC, NESSA, OFELIA, OFELIA, SANDRA, SANDRA
		-- END OF DAY 13 -- Tuesday, August 21, 2018		4 4/8 pgs.	

You'll see that the Wasteground scenes (including Sc. 64) are being shot the day before the more complex Sc. 65 (Day 12) — which is a 'light' 2 5/8ths day to allow for stunts, vehicles and rain-making. Notice also that Day 12 falls on a Sunday. This is a deliberate trick, especially in 'low budget' filmmaking. The intense night shoot (Sc. 65,66) has been scheduled before the Day Off, to give everyone the chance to recover. (Day 11 has a less complex night shoot, but there's been an allowance for a 'late call time' the following day with two short daylight scenes up first).

To summarize: I know this has been a long chapter, but that reflects how vital it is that you understand the nuts and bolts of Scheduling. Get together with whoever creates your Stripboard and carefully go through it. Watch out for days that go way over your Page/Day ratio. If you're supposed to shoot 4 pages a day, but there's a day in the Schedule that adds up to 13 pages, you might want to question that. However, an 8-page day that has three dialogue scenes in a simple location with straightforward lighting and a rehearsed cast is nothing to be too worried about. A day that has one page — but involves a complicated action scene — will be the trade-off for that 8-page day that your A.D. thinks is acceptable.

A couple of 'pro' tips;

- Give yourself an 'easy' start to your production. It takes 3 days for a Crew and Cast to get comfortable and operating at an optimal and fully efficient speed. Make your first couple of days slightly under your normal page/day ratio. Consider everyone's unfamiliarity both with the project and with each other and make time for that. Allow extra time to deal with all the usual minor issues and delays that are a natural part of getting the production up and running smoothly.

- Don't attempt a 'company move' on your first day if you can avoid it. And don't under-estimate what a 'company move' actually is. Moving a mere half-mile from an

Exterior location to the studio where you're filming Interiors for the rest of the day might seem a no-brainer — but you'll lose at least a full hour. (Sneaky Producers make such a 'move' as lunch is being called — thinking that the 'move' can be accomplished in the downtime. This appears to be smart — but some members of the crew will immediately become resentful that their lunch break is being wholly or partially lost in moving their gear and their bodies. And if it turns out that their lunch is allowed to go cold while they make the 'move', you can expect some of them to be on their cellphones looking for other jobs by the end of the day and you'll be scrambling to replace them).

Which reminds me. Crews don't give a damn about your 'passion'. They are not interested in being involved in a 'labor of love'. They have absolutely no motivation to work for Producers or Directors who expect them to 'care' enough about the precious project so as to forgive bad food, poorly-organized schedules, unsafe working practices and inept leadership. To them, it's a job. Nothing more. So, don't behave like a gadfly amateur around experienced professionals. Treat your Crew with respect and look out for their well-being. Do that consistently and you'll quickly gain a positive reputation that extends far beyond the crew personnel you work with. On those tough days (and you will have them) you'll find that a well-cared-for Crew will rally around you and go the extra mile. Film production is a battlefield. A Crew will work their hearts out for a Director who looks out for them — and they will just as happily toss a grenade into the foxhole of the arrogant leader who treats them dismissively.

In Conclusion: Time. Remember? Not your friend. Study your Stripboard. Refer to your script. Make sure that you have not been set up for failure.

- *Set up for failure? Why would anyone do that?*

Because everyone's an optimist. And, sometimes, people who are hired by a Producer imagine that their job is to please the Producer. They seem to be under the impression that the Producer is making the picture. You need to gently disabuse them of this woeful notion. We're not working in episodic television, after all. In their effort to please the Producer, some of the Production Office personnel involved in Scheduling take the view that you just need to get it done. Irrespective of how impossible and crazy that might be.

So, watch out for over-loaded days. Watch out for 'company moves' to locations many miles, and several traffic-choked freeways, apart. Watch out for DAY and NIGHT strips slammed together which will result in lighting changes that will take time and exhaust your crew. Watch out for those little 1/8th page strips thrown into busy days, which turn out to be an 1/8th page of intense action or complicated set-up that will suck up 4 hours of your precious time. Watch out for strips that bunch together emotionally-demanding and dialogue-heavy scenes that will deplete your leading actor's reserves. Watch out for first days in locations that will require difficult lighting or set dressing. Watch out for scenes that have costuming or special make-up changes that require time. Watch out for Schedules that don't take full consideration of how long a 'simple' stunt is going to set-up, rehearse and shoot.

The list of caveats is long. The biggest caveat is this; Don't accept a Schedule unless you are confident that you can perform what is being required of you in the allotted Time.

That's what I mean by 'Selecting for Success'

CHAPTER THREE

Locations

There's a reason I put 'Locations' second on the list of elements that you must select for success. Nothing is harder, especially for the low-to-no-budget filmmaker, than finding locations. It takes time to lock down those locations that are going to be the right ones for your shoot. A lot of time. You need to jump on it really fast.

If a large enough budget is available, you'll have a Location Manager and Location Scouts. The Scouts need your brief and your feedback. Things that look promising, you visit and examine — until that satisfying moment when you find the workable solution. On smaller 'no-budget' shoots, the Producer is the Location Manager and — guess what? — the two of you are likely to be the Location Scouts.

The choice of location begins in your mind. It is filtered through your experience or imagination from the Clues in the script. It either exists in physical availability, or it does not. If not, you're working on a digital backlot, or you're transforming physical space into the 'vision' you have in your head. Everything boils down to bucks. How much money do you have? If you need to create your 'vision' of a street in 1930's Shanghai — is there a place in the world where that exists in physical reality and which your budget makes available, or do you have to either construct a set on a sound-stage in Valencia, California or build it digitally and go shoot on a Green Screen stage in Queens, NY?

Your first job is to have a clear idea of the kind of location that is going to work for the scene. If you need inspiration — go online, bring up the websites for the various Film Commissions or Film Offices in the state (or nation) where you plan to shoot (several US states have both state-wide and local commissions) and trawl through the Location suggestions. If you have no luck, then entering a 'Google' search for the type of location you need can, at the very least, give you a visual reference to show the team.

I attended a location scout recently for a short feature I'm consulting on. The action takes place between two men in a cave. The director wants to shoot in an actual cave. There's a location in the Hollywood Hills that is the 'go-to' cave for filmmakers on a tight budget. We can get the cave. However, the script also calls for the cave to collapse, trapping the two men inside. Much discussion ensued. As "consultant" I pointed out that we could shoot the first part of the film in the actual cave, and then shoot the "collapsed cave" segment on a stage. The DP was in favor of this, but the Director remained unconvinced. He didn't have a large budget, so an attempt to create a "collapsed cave" in a studio, either with a set or using green screen, risked an artificial result. The director wanted his story to be told in a 'realist' manner. So, a choice had to be pondered and a decision made.

This small moment from an actual pre-production meeting brings up a pertinent question. *What kind of filmmaker are you?* Some of us are realists. We set out to tell our stories with the eyes of a documentarist. We can't abide artificiality or anything that seems staged or over-crafted. We want a gritty truth. We want the audience to feel the reality. But some of us work at the other extreme, and our scenes are set in worlds that have been molded into something that is, to a greater or lesser degree, artificially heightened, deliberately removed or completely detached from reality. Of course, there are filmmakers equally at home in both grittily-realist *and* stylized 'formalist' traditions and plenty more who come somewhere in the middle and are equally adept in realist or formalist traditions — many of the "classic" filmmakers from Hollywood's Golden Age could be described that way. For others, the very artificiality of filming something causes it to become overly stylized — and there are filmmakers who fight against that by deliberately taking artifice out of their work. Step forward Monsieur Godard, and all you disciples of *Dogme 95*.

Whether your sensibilities fall into 'Realist' or 'Formalist', it is important that in selecting a film location you understand, as Hitchcock was fond of pointing out, that it cannot merely be a background. Not if you're serious about your craft. Creatively, you need to examine the physical space where you will place the world of your film and figure out if it has everything you need to fully integrate into your story — or if it can be changed, according to your budget, so that it will do the job required. That's the first task. Next is to examine the location for its technical suitability — an easier job. You must be the final arbiter on the suitability of the location just as surely as you need to have the final word on everything else that impacts your creativity. Never accept a location without physically examining it. "Walk the ground". You cannot begin to see how your actors and cameras will move in the space until you go there. Nor can you organize your Shot List (which we will discuss fully in *Shooting The List*) without knowing your locations intimately. The perfect location does not exist, except in your own mind and in the imagination of the screenwriter. Some locations (and studios) can, and should, be dismissed out of hand — they are so obviously wrong no further effort is needed. All the rest need your consideration and input to find the best way of using them to fit the film you are making, whether that's a 'realist' portrayal for a vivid drama story set in NYC, or a deliberately artificial and 'formalist' fantasy played out like a hallucinatory nightmare.

Let's look at your 'Technical' responsibility more closely. As a director, you must be aware that every aspect of the location needs your active appraisal. Sure, there will be people to point out the pros and cons to you, but you can't just ignore the flaws of a location because it meets your 'vision'.

- *Why not? Flaws can be corrected, can't they? I thought you said we could use production resources to make the location "work"? Why can't we just send in the Art Dept. and make whatever changes the 'vision' requires.*

Well, yes. We could do that. Productions are constantly adapting locations to fit the story and the 'vision'. If you have the necessary budget, you can reshape a location just the way it needs to be to meet the demands of the script. Even with no budget, many minor 'flaws' can be overcome by adjusting a camera angle or painting out something inappropriate. Moving an object — or an actor! — to hide a 'flaw' is commonplace. But 'flaws' that can be solved by repositioning or covering up are not what I'm talking about. I'm thinking of the 'flaws' that will kill your shoot, particularly if your production is of the 'micro-budget' variety.

When I first came to America permanently, like most immigrants I took any job I could get. I was crewing on a production in Arizona — we were making a Western — and the Location Department had found an old caboose for a Night Interior Train scene. The director liked the caboose, although the Art Department were having a fit wondering how to turn a 1970's caboose into an 1870's caboose. The Director prevailed. The Location Department smirked and checked that one off their list. A month later, Crew and Cast arrived at the location for our all-night shoot. It was a typical summer's night in southern Arizona. Hot. The Art Department had done a valiant job of removing 'modern' elements from the caboose. The Camera and Lighting Departments squeezed themselves in and gamely set up lights and sticks. The Sound Mixer quickly realized he wouldn't fit on the caboose, so located his gear outside. The Boom Operator struggled to place his shotgun mic out of frame — fighting the low ceiling — and hoped the wireless Lavalier mics attached to the actors would do the job. The heat built up so fast that the Make-Up Department ran into problems keeping the actors faces dry and their make-up in place. The actors got all pissy and upset. The inside of that caboose began to resemble the scene from the old Marx Brothers movie where the cabin of an ocean liner gets crammed with people, each one trying to do their separate job, until the tiny space gets so full the door bursts open and they all fall out. It became, frankly, insane. Finally, with an inside temperature hovering around 115 F, and the A.D. having a nervous breakdown, we were ready to shoot. It was 2 a.m. The Director called 'Action', and at that precise moment the previously unnoticed Jet Engine Testing Plant, located less than 25 yards from the caboose, started its nightly work. Testing a Jet Engine. The noise was so loud, nobody heard the Director yell 'Cut!' Producers and Assistant Directors ran frantically to the Testing Plant, begging them to turn off the noise — and were told to go away and play with their train.

The moral of the story is this. That was One Huge Flaw that someone should have recognized and reported. You might think that this was the Location Department's fault — and, up to a point, you'd be right — but, in the final analysis, the blame must lie with the Director. It's not only the *immediate* location that's important. It's also the surrounding area. As the Director, you cannot ignore the major 'flaw' of a location you're excited about, or not study the situation fully. Nor can you dismiss the concerns of your Department Heads, or the evidence of your own eyes and ears. Don't assume it'll be okay. This is filmmaking. It's never okay.

It is incumbent on you to really push the Location scouting and selection process. Push *hard*. Why? Because, it's your picture and — I repeat — you need to find the possible locations quickly, so you can bring your team in for further inspection and discussion. On larger productions, your visual reference and briefing will send the scouts out and they'll get back with suggestions and photos. Those you like, you'll go and visit. Once again, don't just be the guy who says *'Yes, this matches my precious vision'*. Be the person who studies the location, who's aware of all the issues that your Department Heads will be concerned about. Check if there are going to be problems with access, with location availability, electrical power, suitable points for rigging lights. Inquire about toilet facilities. Ask to see areas set aside for wardrobe and make-up. Find out how many vehicles can be parked.

Yes, yes, I know these are 'Producer Problems' but — trust me in this small matter — *all* problems are 'Director Problems'.

Filled with this new wisdom, you'll be returning to your short-listed or chosen location some days or weeks later for a full 'tech recce' (or 'tech scout') with your team. Sometimes this takes place within a few days or hours of the shoot itself — largely because tight budgets and crew availability prevent earlier inspection. Present will be your Director of Photography (usually with the Electrical Department's Gaffer), your 1st Assistant Director, your Production Designer, your Line Producer and, if necessary, your Stunt Coordinator. Once again, you'll be going through the litany of concerns, some old, some new — areas for parking, for staging equipment, ease of access, ceiling height, availability and type of power, security requirements, placement of catering. Along with sensible questions about how the location will be affected by weather, or the position of the sun. Each Department Head will have a particular concern and sometimes those concerns become "issues" which will require you to rethink your 'vision'. You'll find that every shot you've planned or imagined is scrutinized from multiple angles. The Director of Photography working out how to make the shot and the equipment required, the Gaffer checking on power availability and length of cable runs, the 1st A.D. working out access and potential crowd control problems — and figuring out how long it will take to make the shot so that time can be allocated in the schedule, the Production Designer noting what is required to create the "world" the director is building, the Line Producer keeping everyone grounded and aware of time and budget limitations — and alert to safety and legal issues such as trade-marked brand names, advertising posters, artwork including murals, etc., that might get in the shot and make it unusable.

I didn't mention the Production Sound Mixer — and that person is vital to the success of your shoot — so overrule those who say it's not important for the Sound Mixer to be present for the 'tech scout'. On the original 'location scout' it will have fallen to you, my dear director friend, to be the Sound Mixer's ears and make a judgement regarding the suitability of the location for audio or, at minimum, prepare for the more obvious problems. And what might those problems be? Proximity to Airports and Freeways. Schoolyards. Construction sites. High levels of ambient noise in Interiors — busy streets, subway rumbles, heavy truck and bus-passes, electrical hums, elevators and other mechanical noises. Uncontrolled livestock. Dogs. Geese. Frogs. (Yes, frogs! — as those of us who have shot in Puerto Rico can attest). And Jet Engine Testing Plants. On the 'tech scout' the Sound Mixer will be able to note and make plans for additional issues that perhaps only a specialist can foresee. Ceiling height, for example, which will allow boom poles to be used, or not. Concrete walls and stairwells that will cause 'reverb' and 'echo' that cannot be removed from your production dialogue. Metal steps or wooden floors that make footsteps too prominent and cannot be separated from the dialogue to allow the words spoken to be properly heard. The Sound Mixer has solutions for all these issues — but needs the 'tech scout' to identify and prepare for them.

And you might want to make doubly sure and check with your Line Producer that whoever has the key to the building you want to use, or to the gate you need to open to access the location, is fully aware of the time you intend to arrive, and that someone on your production staff has that person's 24/7 contact information — information which should also be noted on your Call Sheet.

Yes, I know you *think* directors don't need to worry about this kind of thing. That's why I'm telling you this stuff!

CHAPTER FOUR

The Cast

Next up on my list of 'Tasks-To-Jump-On-Immediately' is Casting.

Casting decisions are often nothing to do with the director — (refer once again to the Katie Maratta cartoon). Producers usually find funding because they have specific acting talent attached — and these attachments can be in place long before a director is decided upon and hired.

In that circumstance, it will be the already-cast Leading Actor(s) who will make the decision whether or not to work with a proposed director, not the other way around. For first-time directors this is always tricky, as 'known' and 'bankable' actors, and their agents, have no desire to give over their image, their performance and their careers to the inexperienced. You might be an award-winning television commercials director, or have won prizes for your edgy 20-minute short feature, but in terms of full-length theatrical feature film-making you'll still be regarded as a novice. People are very keen to tell you that there's a big difference between making a 60-sec commercial and a full-length feature film. Although that difference is much slighter than those people imagine, it's a baked-in obstacle to getting your feature film career moving. It's the old story; people are reluctant to give you a job until you've already done the job — or are already incredibly famous in some other creative discipline. If you face this challenge from An Important Actor there are ways to overcome it, but the best is this tasty combo; (i) relying on your (experienced) producer to extol your incredible gifts, (ii) appearing fresh, enthusiastic, collaborative and respectful when meeting the Great Star and (iii) having ownership of a wonderful script. If Important Actors want to work on your script badly enough, they'll accept you as Director provided there's some small evidence of your filmmaking skills. You can cement the deal by already having in place a Cinematographer who is a 'known' professional. Actors get much more relaxed when they know there's someone recognizable heading up the Camera Department. Assuming you're in place, let's move on.

The Casting Director: Yes, even small 'micro-budget' productions occasionally employ the specialized services of a casting director. But a professional casting director does not come cheap, so at the lower end of the budgetary spectrum many producers will feel inclined to take on the job themselves. If that happens, insert yourself into the process very quickly and very firmly —or you'll find yourself having to direct actors that do not match your character concepts or — worse— don't have the performance skills to fully inhabit the role.

Smart, well-funded producers always go to the professional expert. Casting Directors repay their investment because they are able to identify not only which actors will work for the part and the budget but, critically, for the future marketplace. This point is often overlooked. Casting Directors have a very good sense of how a particular actor is going to be perceived by distributors, exhibitors and, by extension, the audience — not merely today or next week, but a year or two into the future. That, by strange and lucky coincidence, is the rough timeframe when your film will be ready to go into distribution. It's going to help your picture in wonderful ways when an emerging star is gathering enough heat to generate interest in their (and your) latest movie.

The best Casting Directors have built their reputation on four main skill-sets;

Skillset #1: They spend their lives identifying which actors, from the vast pool of wannabee talent that parades before them every day of every week, are the ones that will break surface and emerge into the bright sunlight of stardom.

Skillset #2: They are able to read scripts and come up with a variety of suggestions as to the *few* actors that will truly work well in the specific roles on offer. Not in a hit-or-miss, scattershot, 'throw-it-against-the-wall-and-hope-it-sticks' manner, but in a targeted, highly-considered way. Sometimes, those suggestions will surprise, or will be very far from what a director might have first envisioned — but they will have merit.

Skillset #3: The ability, already mentioned, to "read the marketplace" and align the right actor to the role so that when the film is ready for release the interest in that particular actor will be high.

Skillset #4: Perhaps the most obvious. Over the years, Casting Directors build up extensive first-name relationships with Talent Agencies, Artist Managers, Known Stars and Emerging Thespians. They know how to reach out to Actors. You probably don't. Let me just mention that this is a skill you should actively develop. Directors who bring Important Actors to projects get to work more often than Directors who don't. There's many a Director who got a really big step-up in the industry due to a close friendship with an in-demand Actor.

All of that is important, I think you'll agree. So, if the Casting Director is doing all this — what is your job? Simple. Steer the ship.

A Casting Director is your dream date, or your worst nightmare. If (s)he doesn't see the script the way you do — you'll have a problem which may turn into a fight. But most

Casting Directors are very good at what they do and have real empathy with the script. If they're not good, you'll find out very, very quickly. Remember, your best defense is your veto. You may be portrayed as 'difficult' — or worse —but being a Director often requires you to be thick-skinned and protect the project from opinions and choices that are damaging. That doesn't mean you shouldn't be thoughtful and respect the suggestions of your collaborators. Run their idea through your filter and try to be open to what is being offered.

Skillset #2 tells you that a professional Casting Director is presenting someone they have carefully considered is right for the role. Be prepared to have names and faces tossed at you that you can't imagine for the part and try not to dismiss those actors out of hand. You might think that some of the actors being suggested at this time are wildly unsuitable at first glance, but there may be very good 'business' and 'creative' reasons for those suggestions being made. Remember, Casting Directors attend many, many auditions and showcases. They are familiar with actors at all stages in their careers. The best Casting Directors are usually the first to notice and promote a new talent and, the flip side of the coin, are also first to realize when an actor's acceptance in the marketplace is in decline.

A Casting Director once offered me a young actor I hadn't heard of. She was excited about casting him as she'd seen him develop at auditions and 'call-backs' over a two-year period. I took a look at the resume and the headshots — and wasn't impressed because the actor didn't immediately strike me as the *lean and hungry-looking bad boy* I'd imagined for my leading role. The resume confirmed that he'd not played characters that were anywhere near close to the role I was trying to cast. So, I passed on auditioning him. 18 months later, when my film should have been going into release, the young man I had rejected was a household name with his face on every supermarket tabloid in America. The role he was playing to great acclaim?

A lean and hungry-looking bad boy.

I know that a Casting Director is a luxury not every production can afford, but let's imagine we have an extremely wise producer who correctly thinks the expense is worth every cent. What happens now?

First, it will be useful — whether the project has an attached Casting Director or not — to get your concept of the character down on paper (briefly). A two or three sentence description — which may differ in some respects from the script — is helpful to your Producer and to the Casting Director. It should mean that your interpretations of each character don't clash too badly with other key technicians on the team — who, of course, haven't bothered to go to the trouble of developing this 'character brief'. Build a short description for every role — and don't be afraid to suggest actors you think would be suitable.

The Process will begin with casting the leading roles, provided attachments have not already been made.

Some of the actors approached to appear in your movie will never go to an audition or make a video of their interpretation of the offered role for you to peruse at your leisure. Ever. We know these actors by the appellation; 'International Name Recognition Talent'. It is assumed you know their body of work intimately, so auditions are both superfluous and insulting.

When there's a first-time director onboard, the 'Name Talent' casting tends to be the Producer's task, in collaboration with the Casting Director. It's tempting to believe Producers choose 'Name Talent' for monetary and marketing reasons first, and creative reasons long after that. Tempting — because it's often true. Make sure your Producer is aware of how you see the role played and who might play it most interestingly. Your suggestions and thoughts may not carry much weight with a Producer whose primary concern is casting a Star Actor who will appeal to the Bank, the Distributor and the Marketing Department, but some idea you have might penetrate. Better yet, your Producer may think it's her brilliant idea in the first place.

The inclusion of Name Recognition Talent into the Process is usually a major step forward in the film becoming a reality. For you, as a Director who perhaps has never worked with an International Movie Star before, the attachment of a Known Actor is a moment that can feel a little surreal.

As I laid out in the opening to this chapter, it is more than likely that the Actor won't fully commit to making the picture until he or she has met with, and approved, you — the Director. In my career, these meetings have usually taken place at a lunch paid for by the Producer, or over drinks in some quiet and exclusive cocktail bar. 'Meeting-The-Star' appointments that take place in the Star's office, hotel room or home are always more uncomfortable because it's easy to feel that you're intruding into their space — unless they're super friendly and relaxed, which they aren't because the whole purpose of this meeting is to size you up, and actors are often (and surprisingly) shy people who have to make an effort when it comes to meeting people outside their inner circle.

When the moment of being put under the microscope arrives it helps to be sincere and honest in your responses and not try to impress. (Never 'name-drop' — the famous name you brandish might turn out to be someone who is the mortal enemy of the Actor 'auditioning' you). There will be questions about the script. Questions about how you see the character. Perhaps a concern with a particular scene. Maybe a request to make a change. There will likely be a question as to who the Cinematographer is, or who will edit the film and if you've worked with these people before. The Star will have also done some due diligence on you — so expect a question about your previous work and associations. Actors are very sensitive to authenticity — and the Directors I know who are the most "authentic" are the ones who have the best relationships with actors. I mentioned being sincere and honest — and that's the best suggestion I can give you for 'Meeting-The-Star' even if a sincere and honest response might not seem the best approach.

I was once asked by an Extremely Famous Star what my personal opinion was of a film of mine that I knew he'd seen — because the Producer had sent it to him along with a glowing recommendation. I replied that although I was glad most people seemed to like it, I was uncomfortable with the film and felt I could, and should, have done a lot better. Out of the corner of my eye, I saw the Producer get that glazed expression they have when things look like they might start to go south. But the Star just looked at me for what seemed the longest time, then nodded and smiled — and from that moment on we had a rapport.

Another time, I misjudged the room. I thought a Hugely Important Star was enjoying our conversation — and I felt it was important to take the time to explore the ideas and concepts with him. In my naïveté, I thought that turning the meeting into a mini pre-production briefing would be helpful — but 'no'. I learned the next day that he was about to go on a hot date and had wanted the meeting to be over but didn't know how to end the conversation and get me out of his house. He had absolutely no interest in my thoughts, either on the project or his performance, and told his management that I was tiresome and boring. The management had no problem in telling my Producer those interesting facts. No coming back from that one. During filming, the Star treated me with impatience and aloofness and I, in turn, treated him with icy politeness and the utmost brevity.

Something else sometimes happens in these 'Meeting-The-Star' moments. If you're not yet a well-known Director, you may find that the Star doesn't pay much attention to you. Their attention is predominantly on the Producer. After all, this is the person who's going to pay them. To the Actor, at this point, the picture belongs to the Producer. The Producer, in turn, is putting on the charm — it's usually one of their dominant skill sets — so you might begin to feel that the meeting is turning into a love-fest between Producer and Star and you're being excluded to some extent. Don't fret. It's a positive move forward that Star and Producer are beginning to bond, but, ultimately, the bonding should be between you and the Star. This first meeting may not be the moment to establish that bonding. Don't force it. As you sit there, listening to the Star and the Producer swap stories, be aware that the Star is quietly sizing you up. Stay relaxed and present. Don't drink too much or chew with your mouth open. When the Star finally turns to you and engages you with their question or concern — it helps to have a response that shows your confidence, your thoughtfulness and your enthusiasm. If the meeting results in the Star either attaching, or remaining attached, to the project — and you're still the Director — you've passed the audition. The next time you meet the Star — which most probably will be on their first day of shooting — you'll be a familiar face and the bonding and collaboration can begin.

With the heavy lifting of attaching the Leading Roles done, the Casting Director's team gets to work to cast 'Supporting Roles'. They will normally do an initial 'filter' through the 'possibles', organizing auditions, sending out 'Sides' (selected excerpts from the script), reading actors at a casting audition and sending you links to video of those readings. From that you'll make some choices — and the Casting Director will 'call back' selected actors for a second reading. You will be present at the 'callback' — but sometimes you need to be somewhere else (pre-production has huge demands on your availability). If you can't be there and you have specific directions that you would want to give the auditionees — pass that onto the team. Most of the 'Supporting Roles' might be cast at this point, but if some cannot be decided… there's a 'third call-back'. Perhaps more.

Most often, the first time you'll meet your actors is in an audition or 'call-back'. A spooky and unnatural environment where paranoia collides with emotional vulnerability. For your important roles, the Actor knows you're probably only considering a handful of others. They will come in and read with you, listen to you talk about the film, ask a few questions. It's a little strange to suddenly find yourself sitting across a table from someone who's face, voice and mannerisms you are familiar with from countless TV shows and movies — but try not to let it show. The most important question you need to ask yourself is;

- *Can this actor inhabit the character?*

Given that the Actor is a professional, highly skilled performer, a large part of the answer to that question is; *'Yes, of course!'*. But is (s)he the right fit for the part in your mind? Only you can decide if this Actor allows you to *see* the character. If you see only the Actor, then so will the audience. Let me try to amplify that observation. Imagine you are in a brightly-lit room. There's a video camera or iPhone recording everything. An Actor sits opposite you; somewhat nervous perhaps, maybe vastly confident, or relaxed and smiling. Wearing street clothes... (try not to grimace if an Actor appears in what they think is "costume" suitable for the movie — but only those lowest on the ladder to fame will attempt it). If you close your eyes, does the Actor's voice and vocal delivery make you see the character? If so, open your eyes. Can you still see the character? Can that character be glimpsed in the way the Actor is moving his facial muscles, the way his shoulders shift? In your imagination, can the character brought forth by this Actor interact with the other characters in the film? With those already cast? This isn't simple. Sometimes it's a blind leap of faith. An instinct. It's very easy to like the Actor personally and know that you are somewhat of a fan of their work — and think that's sufficient. It's tempting to say to yourself; *"Well, I didn't see the character very clearly, but the actor is solid and that's all that matters."* Unfortunately, that's not true.

Or perhaps the Actor is idiosyncratic, and explosively takes the character somewhere you hadn't imagined? Does it matter? Not if it felt surprisingly correct. As long as you glimpsed, in this fresh perspective and approach, how the character would be formed, then you only need ask yourself this;

- *Will this actor's mannerisms, attached to this character, work in the context of the whole film?*

Some Actors are so uniquely mannered that their on-screen personalities are 'special effects' in themselves. Is yours a movie that would benefit from a 'highly-mannered', idiosyncratic Actor in this specific role? Or will those mannerisms ultimately disengage the audience?

Next, you have to work out whether you can work with the Actor in front of you, in an atmosphere of creative respect, for the time it takes to shoot his/her sequences. I want to be able to enjoy being with my Actors. I want to feel that I could hang out and relax with them, have a drink or a meal and not be stiff and formal and uncomfortable around them. The Actors may want to get the same feeling about you — otherwise you're just their work supervisor — and that's not a great relationship.

These questions have to be answered in the ten minutes allowed before the Producer starts to covertly catch your attention and tap her watch. Be respectful with anyone who auditions for you. Be friendly. Come across as creative and focused and able to listen. Be grateful that they have taken the time to come and read. Do not interrupt and start "directing" them while they're reading, although a short discussion and a request to do a second 'take' is always acceptable.

Auditioning is a very tough thing for an Actor to do at any level in the industry but especially for those who are less experienced. Do not giggle, laugh out loud, moan, groan or pull faces at anything that is presented to you even if it is beyond bad. If you are unsure of an Actor, or sense perhaps that he/she doesn't quite get it — then it's a good idea to suggest or request; "*I like what you just did, but maybe you could try it once more, this time, how about making it just a little lighter?"* The Actor will ask *"Lighter?"* and you'll have to amplify. *"Yeah, as if the character doesn't care quite so much."* See what you get. You will then have a fairly good idea of how well this Actor will respond to direction on the day of the shoot. Nine times out of ten, an inexperienced or poorly-trained Actor will not be able to make *any* subtle or distinct shift in the earlier reading. But even with unknowns you will sometimes get an Actor who will give you exactly what you requested. So, request something else — just to make sure. *"Do you think it would come out different if you were trying to hold back anger?"* An Actor who has come this far won't ask a question like *"Anger? What are you talking about?"* He'll probably say something like, *"You mean, like I'm angry because the other guy's always late — but I can't show that?" "Precisely!"* you reply, making a mental note to cast this person, and then watch as the flexibility asserts itself and the reading is given with an underscore of 'anger'.

The Actors who will be on your shoot for no more than a day or two are much more difficult to assess than the Actors that have substantial roles. Producers tend to think that the casting of the 'Day Players' isn't that important. After all, they only need to say a line or two and they're wrapped in a few hours. I beg to differ. It's the 'Day Players' that can sink you. A line delivered badly. Too much time taken to get that line halfway right. An expression that is not delivered properly. A physicality that just seems 'off'. These are things that take an audience out of your picture. Imagine. You have two leading players in a coffee shop. Mr. Samuel Jackson and Mr. Ryan Gosling, should you be so lucky. They are involved in a breakfast scene heavy with sparkling dialogue and entertaining action. A 'Day Player' — whom the Producer didn't think it was important for you to see during casting (you were extremely busy, after all) — has a minor line to deliver, along with the simple action of refilling a coffee cup for the character played by Mr. Gosling. Unfortunately, you *believed* the Producer when he said that it wasn't important for you to approve the Day Player he'd selected and — to make matters worse — it is only on the day of the shoot that you discover the Producer took the opportunity to ingratiate himself with one of the investors and give the role to that gentleman's lady friend.

Things could work out just fine. Or not. Let's stay with 'not'.

The moral of the story is this, and forgive me if I'm becoming repetitive, but everything that is in your frame is important and if you don't 'select for success' you're going to be dealing with problems that can sink the scene, the film and even your career. Being a Film Director opens you up for an incredible amount of criticism. There are people out there who actively look for things to judge you on. And not in a positive, encouraging way. They will judge you harshly on "your" cinematography, "your" production design, "your" editing, "your" score and, most especially "your" casting. A 'Day Player' who doesn't fit into the scene, who looks incongruous, who isn't able to work to your direction, who can't deliver the line right, who — in short — is so out-of-place or just plain 'wrong' that it hauls your audience out of the picture, isn't just a minor glitch in a scene that soon passes and is gone. It's a mistake that hands those who want to be critical of you a gift that will hang around you like a bad smell for a long, long time. If you didn't bother to 'select for success' and simply went with the flow of other people's agendas, then that miscasting is your fault. Not the Day Player's. Not the Producer's. Not the Investor's. Not even the Casting Director's. Your fault.

The truth is this. The majority of Actors who work in minor roles don't have much in the way of character flexibility. You get what you get. If it's right — cast them. If not, move on. But do so politely. It is absolutely wrong to use the casting session, especially of 'Day Players' and those in minor 'Supporting Roles', to show off your own importance, prestige and power. You're a Director. You might be the Head of the Acting Department, but you are also the Servant of The Actors.

SELECTING FOR SUCCESS | 67

While on the subject of the awesome power you're perceived to have; consider this. We didn't exactly need the #MeToo movement to tell us — because every single one of us has known about it from Day One — but certain Producers and Directors do hit on actors in casting sessions (and anywhere else they get the opportunity) — and that is Dreadful, Unforgivable, Unprofessional and Completely Lacking in Human Decency and Empathy. So, let's do something to prevent it. If you are a male Director, please be considerate and don't populate your casting sessions with men. Use the modest power of the 'honeymoon phase' of your tenure as Director to keep unnecessary people out of the room. Especially "Investors", "Executives", "Associate Producers" and others who just want to ogle attractive young women.

The less-well-known counterpoint is that Directors sometimes experience thespians 'coming on' to them during casting. It sounds like sleazy fiction, but aspiring Actors and Actresses who sit opposite Directors and Producers and make it obvious that they are 'interested' (sometimes in the most blatant ways) are not unknown in the world's film capitals.

I don't react well to those situations. I feel disrespected and 'used'. Rather like young actresses do when they have to audition to a roomful of drooling guys, or put up with overweight, balding gentlemen whispering improper suggestions to them as they try to leave the room.

Alright. We have a Cast. What next?

Rehearsals and 'Table Reads'? You might not get them. Working actors have busy schedules. It's not uncommon for an actor to be finishing a movie as yours goes into production. They join your shoot once it's well under way. With Important Actors all you might get is a lunch meeting and a chance to talk very generally about the script. These meetings are only useful to establish some kind of rapport with the Actor — and help you get over your nervousness of being in the presence of the

Great. 'Supporting Roles' have busy schedules too — which makes attendance at a Table Read impossible. Your 'Day Players'? Chances are they have 'day jobs'.

A 'Table Read' is exactly as it sounds. It's the process of gathering the cast together around a table and reading through the entire script. I've known Tables Reads to happen during the development phase, when only a few of the cast have been attached and 'stand-in' actors are brought in to fill in the uncast roles. This kind of Table Read is mostly for the benefit of the writer(s), producer(s) and investor(s) so they can see where the project is going and make notes.

However, an actual pre-production 'Table Read' is, in many respects, the beginning of production itself — especially in television (where it is sometimes referred to as the 'Director's Rehearsal'). All the cast are present. Each seat at the table has a printed card with the name of the Actor and the role being played. There's water and snacks and a well-lit room. The Director sits amongst the cast and usually reads aloud the 'Sluglines' and 'Action' paragraphs. Interested and authorized parties, such as Producers and Writers, sit outside the creative circle at the edges of the room. (A first and telling example of the Writer being gently removed from the collaborative process). Everything proceeds good-naturedly with a building sense of excitement that in a day or two these same lines are going to be said 'on set' and 'on camera'.

Feature films are slightly different, as I've noted, because few of the Actors are going to be available, unless they've been contracted and scheduled for paid rehearsal days (and a 'Table Read' counts as a rehearsal day). If Actors *are* available — and are not on another production or living in another part of the country — you stand quite a good chance of having a Table Read and either you or a Production Assistant can stand in for anyone absent. In low budget (non-union) production, even if they're not getting paid, most actors are quite happy to get together at some point before the shoot to read through the script.

But, while there are plenty of Producers, Writers and Directors who *want* to conduct 'Table Reads' — not every Director likes to work that way.

Why? Because not everything that happens at a 'Table Read' is good. It can be an unpleasant, even an unnerving, experience for an Actor to sit around a table, often with people he's never met before, and launch into a role cold. Actors are very vulnerable in these situations. The slightest giggle (at an attempted accent or a vocal mannerism), the merest groan (at a fumble or a too-obvious question) and you've got very real problems on your hands. Insecurities and anxieties will flourish. So too can backbiting, jealousies and the potential for emotional mayhem.

As if this weren't bad enough, there's another reason why 'Table Reads' may not be a good idea. There are Directors who feel —and I'm one of them — that 'Table Reads' and rehearsal schedules have their place in theatre and television but not in feature films. 'Table Reads' and rehearsals tend to rob performance of spontaneous discovery, of serendipity, of emotional freshness. I'm speaking generally here, of course, because some scripts have very complex and lengthy dialogue scenes that do require rehearsal. Oh, wait. Those are usually screen-adapted stage plays!

To my mind, the true purpose of the 'Table Read' is for everyone to get to know each other, break the ice, and read the entire script so that they understand what kind of film they are working on. It is also the Director's opportunity to establish a safe, courteous and creative environment. I emphasize that a Director, both in television and feature film — but especially in television — is the Head of the Acting Department. It is the Director's duty to make sure a respectful atmosphere is present whenever the cast is gathered. All Actors should be made to feel comfortable in giving their best, and in, ultimately, producing fireworks. More importantly, they should not be made to feel 'judged' because they are holding back (and a word on that in a moment) or giving a performance that is taking them out of their comfort zone. The bottom line is this; at the end of a 'Table Read', the Actors should be warmly looking forward to working with "their" Director.

Here's some suggestions for success.

Make the Actors feel that this is a private, unrecorded and relaxed read-through of the script; *"So we all know the entire story, not just our own parts"*.

Let the Actors know that you want them to read for the sense of the words, not the full emotional performance. *"I want to save what you've got inside for the set"*.

Find ways to let everyone know how much you're enjoying just being with them. Smiles, chuckles at funny lines, nodding wisely at serious bits, being "caught up in the moment" when an actor finishes an important speech.

Keep the flow going. If you must stop to explain how certain things will work during production, then be brief and be inclusive; *"We'll find a way to make it work..."*

If an Actor raises a minor point or question, then by all means answer it then and there. Sometimes, however, a question might arise that is going to stop the flow because it is not a question that can be answered briefly or off-the-cuff. The kind of question, most often, as to how the Actor interprets the role. This situation calls for a judgment call on your part, because you don't want to launch into that kind of intimate discussion with the entire cast listening. Someone may find it too tempting not to voice *their* opinion! Generally, it's best to tell the Actor that you'd like to discuss their question with them during...

The Coffee Break: Ah, coffee. Such a force for civilized discussion and sharpened intellect. Here's your opportunity to informally discuss questions with cast members in a small group or individual basis. You're not 'on set', but you are very much the Director and you are accessible to your cast in ways that seldom happen during production.

In a coffee break or similar situation, if Actors have questions, it helps to 'Be Vague'. I know this sounds counter-intuitive, but your job is to gently allow an Actor to find the answer to their own question. Never be a dictator. Never demonstrate. Ask. Inquire. If you must — suggest.

"What do you think she'd be feeling?"
"Do you think there's something in the character's past we don't know about yet?"
"Maybe the character's feeling uncomfortable with this? Perhaps he sees this as a challenge?"
"Do you think it might...", "Maybe there could be..."
"I wonder if..."

All these phrases trigger the Actor into thought processes that will likely result in them making an interesting choice — and, just as importantly, they'll start to discover that they are collaborating with you — not merely being your robot. Don't overdo it or you'll start to sound much too precious. And artsy. Talk like this 'on set' and the crew might get nauseous.

In fact, the 'Be Vague' rule does not apply 'on set' where there is a Time Pressure. During filming, it helps to be very precise — but always in the context of not giving too much. It works best by dropping a word or phrase that will spark the intent you are looking for.

However, if an Actor comes up to you in the coffee break and says, *'Can I talk to you about my part?'* you will nod instantly, murmur *'Of course',* and lead them to a place where you can both talk without being overheard or observed. This is a vital piece of advice. When Actors want to speak about their part, you should instantly concur with their request. (Unless circumstances make it absolutely impossible in which case you should point out that absolute impossibility and arrange to talk at the earliest opportunity.) You see, *'Can I talk to you about my part?'* is not a casual question. It's an alarm. A clarion call of emergency. Pay attention and take appropriate action. Once you have found a quiet place to talk and the Actor begins to tell you their tale — you must simply listen. They don't want answers! They want to be told that they're on the right path! The *'Can I talk to you about my part?'* question is all about security. Or rather, insecurity. The Actor has been afflicted, temporarily we hope, with Imposter Syndrome. He or she needs to know that they're 'okay'; not a dumb idiot who lucked into this part by some fluke. They need to hear you say that you think they're doing a wonderful job and you respect what they're doing. If there is a specific difficulty — listen for it and don't ignore it. Deal with it, because the Actor is already upset and needs your reassurance. If you shrug and walk away, or dismiss the Actor's anxiety, you're setting yourself up for an unhappy shoot with a disgruntled, insecure, anxious and insecure (yes, it bears repeating) Actor playing one of your roles.

A final word about 'Table Reads'. Sometimes an Actor will give nothing. Not a glimmer of the performance that you are seeking. The inexperienced Producer/Director team starts to sweat and wonders if there's still time to recast. If you know nothing about the Actor, and especially if this is his/her first film, then use that coffee break to make them relax — and make it known that it's safe to take more risks.

However, if an experienced Actor, who has been known for great performances, gives nothing in rehearsal then she's saving it for the day. Expect fireworks. It's said that the Great British Actor, Sir Laurence Olivier, found that if he made the first read-through a full performance, it took weeks of rehearsal to get back to that raw honesty and emotion. He let it rip on camera, not at a 'Table Read'. There are also Actors who have minimal energy —both during the 'Table Read' and 'on set'. You really have to have seen this Actor's previous work to reassure yourself or you're going to be very nervous on the first day of shooting. Remember also that an Actor is interpreting the script. If there is nothing showy and full of drama in the script — why should a naturalistic Actor invest it with a power and energy it doesn't need or deserve?

Once again, Full Cast 'Table Reads' in pre-production are not as common as you might think. More often than not the cast cannot be assembled at one time and in one place. Ever. Not even during shooting. And 'Table Reads' during script development are really only useful to Writers to help sharpen the script and seldom have the actual cast present. Given that you can still make a wonderful film without a 'Table Read' — why risk it? Some Directors hate the whole idea of letting the Actors read through the entire script. It might give them too many ideas. And there's more than a few Actors who will never read the complete script – just their own lines. There are even Directors who will not give the Actors scripts at all — which I would consider borderline sadism.

My own rule is this: If the film is an ensemble piece, in which the connection between characters and their interaction is of paramount importance — 'Table Read' it for sure, and then rehearse the more complex scenes in a spirit of discovery and full revelation of meaning — but only if you have the time, the availability of cast, and the budget for rehearsal. If it's an action-driven story, in which characters are woven into the action — and the script is full of small moments of dialogue – forget the 'Table Read'. Rehearse the tricky action moments only — the wire work, the sword fights, the tango sequence.

- *Does this mean that actors may arrive 'on-set' without any rehearsal at all?*

Yes. Especially in 'low budget' filmmaking. Rehearsal takes place before the shot is made.

There are two basic production rehearsal procedures (not counting any work you might have done 'off-set' while things are being set up — a read-thru of the lines in the make-up trailer, for example). Those two 'basic' procedures are 'The Walk-Thru' followed, or proceeded by, "Blocking". I won't spend much time here discussing pre-production rehearsal or 'blocking'. This will be dealt with completely in Vol. 6 of T*he Filmmaker's Art* series, *Actors On Set*. But, let's imagine you've started to set up for the next scene. Your A.D. has brought two actors onto the set — often prior to them going into MUAH. You explain the shot and their positioning. '*Joe, you sit behind the desk... and Jill, you'll come in, but instead of sitting down you'll go to the window and look out for a long beat... before your line. Okay? Let's take a look at it.*' While the crew looks on (principally; cinematographer, lighting gaffer, best boy, script supervisor, key grip, assistant director, set dresser, props master) the actors go through the motions you've indicated, moving from one 'block' to another. If problems arise, and adjustments required, they are noted and fixed.

Now, it could well be that the 'Walk-Thru' is a complete mess — it looks awkward and unnatural, the actors don't feel comfortable, the technicians are noticing all kinds of issues that will have to be dealt with. So, you move onto 'Blocking' — and fine tune the movements and the positioning until it is working.

That is how the majority of directors stage a scene.

Following the 'Walk-Thru', the actors are sent back to MUAH. They now know how they'll be moving in the space, and where they're going to be throughout the scene in relation to the camera and the other performers. Having seen the 'Blocking'/'Walk-Thru', the crew gets busy on final preparations to make the shot(s). When the actors return, fully costumed and in make-up, there may be a final rehearsal prior to the shot being made — so that actors and crew can get fully comfortable with what is required. (Many directors shoot this rehearsal, sometimes without mentioning to the actors that the camera is rolling).

Suffice to say, during production — if you haven't carefully prepared how you will shoot a scene — 'blocking' can become time-consuming and difficult, largely because it's taking place with performers that you may never have worked with before, in a workspace that may be completely unfamiliar, on a set or location cluttered with cables and film equipment and requiring the use of unfamiliar props and practical set-dressing elements like doors, chairs, lights, windows and miscellaneous children or animals.

And it has to be done it in full view of a crew who will be carefully watching how effective your directorial skills are.

Thus, 'rehearsal' or 'blocking' of a scene in pre-production may be advantageous when there's a combination of complex dialogue and physical movement. In effect, you do what in theatre would be described as a 'technical rehearsal', so that you and your actors can move like a well-oiled machine during the future production 'Walk-Thru' and easily deal with the minor unexpected issues that may arise 'on-set'.

The classic, over-reached example of 'pre-production blocking' is Hitchcock's *Rope* (1948) — a film (adapted from a stage-play) shot in continuity with ten separate set-ups (well, almost). The actors had to rehearse the entire script, with the technicians working lights, camera and the set itself around them. Everybody and everything had to be perfectly timed and positioned. You're unlikely to require that depth of preparation, but if you have something complicated it helps to have your Cinematographer present at a rehearsal to watch your 'pre-production blocking' so that she understands how best to light the scene and how the camera will be positioned and will move relative to the actors.

A more contemporary film that required intense levels of both pre-production and 'on-set' production rehearsal is the direct descendent of Hitchcock's *Rope* (MGM,1948). A film that, like *Rope*, "appears" to be shot in a single continuous 'take'. I'm referring, of course, to Sam Mendes' remarkable *1917* (Universal, 2019). The choreography between camera and actor(s) present in that film is not something that could be done 'on the fly'. Somewhere between four and six months of pre-production technical rehearsal was required — most of it on the actual set-built locations. (Which had been pre-modelled extensively to gauge necessary dimensions for cast and camera choreography and for lighting design). In principal photography, multiple takes were made of each shot — the longest being seven minutes. Again, very much in the same way — although on a hugely grander scale — that Hitchcock employed on *Rope*.

Yes, it's fair to say that if you are fortunate enough to helm a project of *1917*'s magnitude, with its inherent technical challenges — you're going to be rehearsing until you drop. But you're also going to have the best technicians in the world by your side — production designers like Dennis Gassner on your team, and a cinematographer like Roger Deakins to help you climb Everest.

Chances are, however, that your first films won't be as grand as *1917*. Because of that, actor availability, time constraints and budget limitations will severely limit the amount of rehearsal you can expect.

But don't let that alarm you unduly. One of cinema's greatest Directors — and the most actor-astute — has this to say about rehearsal.

You have to work together with the actors (in film as opposed to stage) in a very emotional, intuitive way at every moment. You use very few rehearsals and, if possible, very few takes, because the actor, when we are making or shooting a picture, he is absolutely open. He works intuitively, creatively, just in the moment. If I want him to repeat what he has made two days later, he can't." — Ingmar Bergman

CHAPTER FIVE

The Look

You're on the way to finding the right locations and assembling your final cast. If it hasn't already happened, in the near future a decision is going to be made on who will be the Cinematographer and Production Designer. You need to start thinking about what your completed film will look like because, whether you've realized it or not, your movie is going to have a 'Look'.

Now, some Directors are more about performance and literary qualities than the visual. And that's okay. They prefer to leave the 'Look' of their picture to the Cinematographer and (in post-production) the Colorist. But to build a signature body of work, don't let a lack of confidence in your visual acuity result in you passing the entire responsibility onto people who may be more knowledgeable and expert. It's better to have a plan, even if it's not a fully conceived plan. In this chapter we'll walk through the stages of developing a 'Look'. Starting with...

The Frame.

If we take a casual glance at most 'Art', we find it has a frame around it. In theatre, that frame is (usually) the Proscenium arch through which we view the stage. Every fine art painting you ever saw has a frame around it.

Film, Television, Streaming Content. iPhone video?

Framed.

We'll leave the discussion on Frame as it relates to Composition for another title in this series. Here, I'm going to discuss the Frame as it relates to the 'Look'. If it's true, and it is, that the only thing that's important in filmmaking is what is in the Frame and everything else — *everything* — is irrelevant, then there's a lot of work to do to make sure that your 'Look' is achieved fully.

Clearly, Cinematography, Lighting and Production Design contribute heavily to the 'Look', but so too does Location, Costuming, Make-up & Hair, Set-Building and Set-Dressing, Props, and (in Post-Production) Color Grading. Can you begin to see how in Pre-Production things begin to pile up, and decisions made in one area immediately affect the others?

Filmmakers often forget that *all* these elements are important, and the result is a 'Look' which seems thrown together. Why? Because it lacks cohesion. It's not unified. Elements appear in the Frame that seems inconsistent or plain wrong. There's absolutely no point in developing a 'Look' that is primarily to do with the Lighting and the Set Design and then putting an Actor in a costume or giving her a hairstyle (or hair color), that does not compliment the overall concept.

'Looks' evolve over time, usually driven by technology and always in support of the story-telling. In previous decades, to give a couple of easily recognizable examples, Technicolor and similar processes brought audiences intense lush colors — perfect for lavish musicals, extravagant fantasies and widescreen epics. And we're all familiar with the direct opposite — the low-key, high contrast 'Look' of 1940s & 50s classic 'Films Noir'. A 'Look' that perfectly complimented the stories being told.

Next time you watch one of the classic vintage Technicolor films, watch out for the name 'Natalie Kalmus' in the end credits. Her credit usually reads 'Color Supervisor' or 'Color Director'. Mrs. Kalmus was the wife of the founder of Technicolor and for almost two decades filmmakers couldn't use the Technicolor process unless they also hired Mrs. Kalmus as a technical consultant. At the time, this drove several prominent Directors, Producers and Cinematographers quietly mad, because they had to bend to Mrs. Kalmus' imperial will. The way she saw it, her job was to protect the Technicolor process and not allow over-enthusiastic arty types to do things with the 'Look' that would tarnish the brand. Naturally, that kind of conservatism led to a tendency to be 'safe' and 'neutral'. It's surprising, then, that the early Technicolor films are so vibrant and have such powerful color juxtapositions. But look more closely. Films like *Gone With The Wind* (1939) or *Meet Me In St. Louis* (1944*)*, while highly color-saturated, have a great many neutral elements to balance the colorful costuming and tone things down before they get too "modern". On the other hand, if you come across a Technicolor film that goes wild to the point where the color of sets and costumes have a kinetic energy — chances are the film was made after 1948 when Mrs. Kalmus' relationship with Technicolor was severed and Associate Color Consultants like Richard Mueller and James Gooch moved into the top slots on pictures like *Singin' In The Rain* (MGM,1952). In contrast to the wildly kinetic color palette of that MGM production, take a look at *Shane* (Paramount, 1953). Director George Stevens and Cinematographer Loyal Griggs' vistas are huge and immensely colorful, but with Richard Mueller's collaboration and guidance, the film doesn't have the artificial quality of earlier Technicolor films. It's much more natural and realist — albeit gorgeously realist.

- *What does this demonstrate, suggest and tell us?*

It demonstrates that whatever is in the Frame can be controlled and the technology manipulated. It suggests that even in what is supposed to be a highly collaborative environment, a commanding individual like Natalie Kalmus can force a

'Look'. It tells us that unless you're prepared to put some work into formulating *your* 'vision' for that Look — albeit in collaboration — then somebody else will take over the task, and you'll have given up an important part of your creative process.

In mainstream film-making today, there are several broadly identifiable 'Looks', and each is fit for genre.

Rom-Com has a warm, sunlit, fresh and colorful look. It's predominantly light and cheerful. Night scenes are glossy and feel glamorous.

Horror has a graduated tonal look that has slightly antiquated blacks and browns, and very often bluish grays and a monochrome feel.

Several Action Thriller and Spy movies also move towards the monochromatic, with a very limited and narrow tonal range. This lends a gritty, subdued mood filled with tension and the potential for danger.

Most current blockbuster Action Adventure movies explore the opposite territory. They have a wide color range that is fresh and highly animated. It's a 'Look' that depends on the principle of 'complimentary color' palettes that allow the actors to 'pop' out of the background and give a very dynamic and super-reality feel to the image. Although I'll be discussing this more fully in yet another fine book in *The Filmmaker's Art* series, you should know that the principal of 'complimentary color' is essentially one of opposites.

Here's an experiment that's fun. Sit in a room with a white or off-white wall. Don't look at the wall. Instead, concentrate on an object or fabric that has a single solid color. Red or Green works best. You could use a piece of brightly colored card, or a sheet of colored paper. Stare fixedly for a good two or three minutes. Now look at the wall. You will see a shape that approximates your card or paper. If the card was red, you will see green on the wall — and vice-versa.

'Okay', you say. *'Nice parlor trick. And how does this help us, exactly?'*

I draw your attention to the work of Vincent Van Gogh. Full of complimentary colors. Vast areas of Orange set against dark Blue. Reds alongside Greens. Bright yellow landscapes under light Blue skies. Result? Vibrancy. Impact. Action. Your brain has become excited.

Translate the concept to cinema. Specifically, Action Adventure cinema. We want our heroic Actors to pop out from the background. The audience is looking at the famous Actor's face. Everything else is secondary. What is the basic color of the Actor's skin tone as it will appear in the final color-corrected film? Clearly, we want the Actor to look healthy — and so Caucasian actors will have a skin tone which veers towards the slightly orange. The 'complimentary color' is muted Green — 'teal', 'sea-green'. Thus, if the Actor wears a 'teal' or 'bluish-green' shirt and is placed against a grey-green background — he will 'pop' out of the screen. Very dramatic, very fresh, very present. And it's not just the thespian elements. Check out the big robots or mechanical monsters. They are particularly useful, as they can be presented in a variety of primary colors or tonal opposites that 'compliment' the other human and environmental elements in the scene.

But, before we rush onwards, let's take a quick step back and realize that a 'Look' has a technical element to it. In the next chapter we're going to meet the Key Creatives who will execute your film's visual design. While everything we've discussed so far is going to be helpful in pre-production meetings with those Key Creatives, it's the meeting with the Cinematographer that may be the most challenging to an emerging filmmaker. Because Cinematography plays such an important part in your 'Look' and because having a deeper understanding allows you to ask better questions, let's take a dive into some aspects of the 'technical' and explore how your choices will affect outcomes.

In the days of film negative, the camera you used wasn't of much importance, other than the format it was capable of shooting (8mm, Super 8mm, 16mm, Super 16mm, 35mm, Super 35mm, 65mm) and the reputation for reliability and precision that a particular manufacturer offered. What was important to a Director and Cinematographer was the film stock used — the negative that would run through the camera. Each manufacturer offered distinct differences and advantages. For example, if your project was mostly Interiors and it was important to have accurate and pleasing flesh tones — then you'd probably go with an Eastman Kodak film stock. If you were doing an outdoors movie, with on-water or oceanside locations, (and your budget was a little tight) then you'd likely choose a Fuji film stock — because Fuji was stellar in their renditions of blues (and any color that 'held' a blue tone - such as teals, and sea-greens). If you wanted a documentary 'Look', with lots of contrast, an ability to shoot in many different lighting conditions and a desire to keep your negative costs down, then you might want to go with Agfa.

Further to the differences between brands, each film manufacturer offered a variety of 'stocks', so it was an advantage for filmmakers to know, for example, that Eastman Kodak EXR 50D 5245/7245 was a low speed 'daylight' stock for 35mm/16mm — a stock with an incredibly fine grain which would give crystal-clear, sharp images and accurate color rendition. Eastman Kodak EXR 100T, on the other hand, was a 35mm stock primarily designed to use with tungsten lighting. It would also produce very 'fine grain' images and would cut together with 5245 without jarring the eye. So, if you were shooting a film which combined sunlit daylight exteriors with day and night *interiors* that would be lit 'tungsten' — and your 'Look' required a glossy, balanced perfection with accurate and pleasing depth of color — then you and your Cinematographer would order up both these stocks on your way to getting the final 'Look'. Of course, for a Director it wasn't necessary to know stock numbers by heart — but it was necessary to understand the benefits and disadvantages of various stocks and how they would affect the 'Look'.

You might be wondering why I should make any mention of film stock at all, given that almost everything today is 'digital' and can be endlessly manipulated.

The answer is that it would be remiss of me not to mention film stock in a chapter on the 'Look'. A surprising number of productions still shoot on actual film negative, despite its expense, its unwieldy nature, its need for careful handling and the high levels of knowledge and expertise involved. Given that demand plummeted in the past decade, some of the once-proud brand names have gone. Kodak remains with a variety of 'stocks' available under their VISION series label. Fujifilm has the ETERNA series — which delivers sharp, highly saturated color images. You will get a very good idea of what available stocks are capable of with some basic research on the internet — 'examples of motion picture film stocks' will bring up video that will be more helpful and inspirational than any words that I can add.

But, let's not kid ourselves. Film is going to go away. Cinemas have, for the most part, converted to digital exhibition. Some filmmakers may continue to originate on film — but the 'release print' will be digital. The "old" film stocks and processes can be digitally recreated — and that technology will only get better — so creating specific film stock 'Looks', even if those 'looks' are "vintage" and no longer exist, will be part of the filmmaker's palette.

So, if we no longer need — as Directors — a basic knowledge of what various film stocks do; what becomes important?

The Camera.

Why? Because the sensor that captures your images differs from camera to camera. And that difference creates a specific and unique 'Look'.

Yes, you could shoot the same material with two completely different cameras and in post-production you could 'tweak' those images so that they ultimately appear to be the 'same'. They won't be — but they'll be close enough. However, the overriding factor is a little thing called 'Dynamic Range' (the ability of the camera to capture light and shadow) and the camera's capabilities in 'Color Management'. If the sensor in one camera can capture images with a dynamic range of 14 stops and another equally fine camera has a dynamic range of 12 stops — then post-production 'tweaking' can get images from both cameras that are identical enough to satisfy most viewers — but the camera with the higher dynamic range will always have blacker 'blacks' and whiter 'whites' because the sensor "sees" better into both dark shadow and bright light.

That doesn't mean that you necessarily need to have a camera with the "best" dynamic range. You may like the way a Canon EOS C700 renders certain colors, or how a Blackmagic Design URSA Mini produces an image with a quality which compliments the story you are telling. Again, the web world has endless camera reviews and video comparisons, so it's not hard to find something that catches your eye and inspires your enthusiasm.

The problem with Cinematography is that it's a deep rabbit hole. For Directors, knowing enough about the subject to be confident in communicating a 'Look' is hard — which is why Cinematographers are usually adept at 'hand-holding'. But, as the host on a popular British quiz show used to say; *'I've started, so I'll finish....'* — and so I will attempt to give you a final, brief pointer for both your awareness and your research.

People get very excited about comparing cameras and their sensors, pointing to 'log curves' and 'codecs'. And that's just dandy. But your pre-production dive into deciding on a camera that meets your creative and budgetary needs requires you to *also* consider the camera's most important component — the lens. I'm not talking about the various focal lengths of the lenses that will be in your camera package (we'll get to that later in the series), nor am I talking about the good, better, best "quality" of those lenses. I'm talking about the interesting fact that a particular set of lenses will uniquely produce a certain 'feel' or 'character' to the captured image — and that 'feel' or 'character' has a large bearing on your 'Look'. It's easy enough to research, for example, world-class prime cinema lenses like Arri Ultras or Zeiss Supremes and find footage online that will give you a very good idea of what those lenses offer. Go a little deeper and you'll start to see the difference between Cookes and Kowas, Hawks and Optica S7 Elites. Lens testing footage abounds once you start to look — but, be careful, you're sure to fall in and out of love. Currently, I'm having a passionate affair with the aforesaid Optica S7 Elites.

To sum up what I realize might seem to be an overwhelming and difficult topic; Your task in pre-production is to explore potential 'Looks', while being fully conscious of the genre of film you are making, and the story being told. Guess what? If you do the research and watch test and comparison videos of cameras and lenses, you will be able to have a very collaborative discussion with your chosen Cinematographer. (You'll also find it easier to evaluate the potential Cinematographers that your Producer may parade in front of you in the early days of Pre-Production crew selection).

Your 'vision' will gradually become more defined as ideas flow, conversations develop, and decisions become more concrete. You'll probably want to continue building a portfolio of images, sketches, fabrics, color palettes and visual aids throughout your pre-production phase. That portfolio (which some call a 'Look Book' — although the same term is sometimes used for a preliminary showcase document during development which, just to confuse us, is also referred to as a 'Deck') is incredibly useful to keep the 'vision' on track and to encourage and inspire your team.

Many Directors take the 'Look' portfolio into production to share with actors and crew or have a 'Mood Board' that illustrates the ambience and palette that will predominate.

A team of key creatives who understand where you're going will make a cohesive, unified picture and be able to bring their skills more fully into the project. Ideally, everybody has to be on the same page, because your 'Look' has to translate to *everything* in the frame.

It bears repeating. A decision regarding a specific 'Look' affects not just the camera package, the color palette and the lighting, but the locations you chose, the costuming you rent or make, the skin tones and hair color of your actors, the sets you build, the props you use.

If it's in the Frame; it is contributing to your 'Look'. One false note — not deliberately and consciously made for a story reason — and your 'Look' is toast.

CHAPTER SIX

The Visual Design Team

There are three key creative/technical persons most responsible for your 'Look'. (i) Your Cinematographer, (ii) Your Production Designer and iii) Your Costume Designer. This is the core of your Visual Design Team.

Your meeting(s) with the Cinematographer and the Production Designer will be the most creatively intense, while many Directors might feel themselves lacking experience and know-how when collaborating with a Costume Designer. But, for the majority of new Directors, the most intimidating meeting you will take during Pre-Production — not counting the Major Star and the Completion Bond Company — is with the Cinematographer. So, we'll start there.

The Cinematographer has the job of actually shooting the film. It's a huge responsibility to build a cohesive, unified visual experience from hundreds of different shots. Every set-up made in the course of production varies in terms of the balance and intensity of light, the ease or difficulty of achieving accurate focus, the cinematic challenges of both stasis and motion, and the best and most interesting use of angle and composition. Cinematography is an immense job, requiring in-depth technical knowledge, years of experience and an absolute mastery of craft.

Let's imagine that you've been asked to select, sometimes with your Producer's gentle guidance, your Cinematographer — perhaps from a long list of very talented people from which you hope to find somebody you can work with successfully and collaboratively. You going to watch a lot a demo reels, and probably narrow it down to 2 or 3 persons to meet with and discuss your project. Unless you're older than I am, and not many people are, you are meeting a person who has much more filmmaking experience than you and whose work you are more than a little awed by. First off, it's far better to be humble than to hide behind a veneer of arrogance. You don't know everything, you don't have the experience — yet —so it behooves you to be willing to ask questions and to learn.

Many of us find it difficult to communicate concepts. To counter that, go into those early meetings prepared to reference movies that have something of the 'Look' you envision. And not just movies. Any kind of visual representation is going to be useful. If you can draw, then do some quick sketches of how you see certain shots being framed. Writing a short visual treatment is useful too — you'll find your ideas becoming clearer. With written or visual references of any kind, you're kick-starting the conversation and you're giving the Cinematographer information she can interpret and plan for.

In a first meeting with the chosen Cinematographer, provided he or she has had a chance to read the script, the discussion might be quite general. You may find yourself discussing the atmosphere or mood of particular scenes or giving an overall concept of how the story develops in terms of the season, the weather, the time of day. Maybe you'll find yourself explaining how the characters develop in terms of their 'arc' and how that might be reflected in the way they are photographed. There are sure to be areas in the script, certain scenes or sequences, where you're not sure how to capture what your instincts are reaching for. Perhaps you know that a certain scene needs complex fast motion and non-standard camera angles to properly convey what the script demands — but you don't know what the technical and equipment

SELECTING FOR SUCCESS | 89

requirements might be. That doesn't matter. Your Cinematographer will have suggestions and explanations. By the end of that first meeting you will either be (a) feeling very confident that you've got the right person for the job or (b) wondering how to tell the Producer that your comfort level with the Cinematographer isn't very high. We hope for (a), in the knowledge that most times (b) proves to be an unfounded fear.

The positive aspects of your relationship with a Cinematographer are beyond measure. When a good Director and a great Cinematographer get together — magic can happen. In the course of your career, I hope you will experience, as I have, the ease and creative satisfaction that comes from working with Cinematographers with whom you are completely 'in sync'. However, it is my unhappy duty to report that not all Cinematographers are going to be a joy to work with. There exists a minority who find themselves to be so special, and who hold themselves in such high regard, that they define the word 'arrogance'. I break these Key Creatives into two 'Difficult' types. First, the incredibly talented and ultra-experienced. Second, the deeply untalented and minimally experienced. They sound very far apart on the spectrum, but their 'Difficult' behaviors emanate from much the same sources.

A Director of Photography is, in the eyes of most of the Crew, many of the Producers, a multitude of Actors and even casual observers, *the single most important person on a film set.* There. I said it. The majority of Cinematographers know that this isn't so. But a significant number have come to believe it. 'On set', Cinematographers are catered to, listened to, obeyed, accommodated, treated with utmost consideration and generally regarded as The Source of All Wisdom. Even Major Movie Stars behave with humility and respect in the presence of the D.P. With the occasional notable exception. Step forward Mr. Bale!

At some point in their distinguished career, 'Difficult DP Type 1' (Talented/Experienced) becomes the kind of rock star who has gotten so used to adulation, and slavish agreement with everything he suggests, that he treats everyone dismissively except those who are bigger rock stars than he. The amusing follow-on is that a creatively frustrated Cinematographer who falls into the 'Difficult DP Type 1' category often aspires to be a Director. All those who have suborned themselves to his imperial presence readily confirm him in this delusional ambition. Disaster lurks. Cinema is littered with the attempts of 'Difficult DP Type 1' to transition to the Director's chair. Many try once and then quickly revert to what they're good at. First, they find out that their genius visual skills are not enough to carry them through in a medium that requires a very deep understanding of literary and performance crafts. They also discover that awe and respect is not given by right to a Director in the same way it is to a Cinematographer. Directors have to earn their place in the sun and prove that they are worthy. Everyone on the set (with the exception of the 1st Camera Assistant) knows for certain that they are *not*, and never will be, a Director of Photography. Yet every single one of those same people is convinced that they could be an outstanding Film Director with thirty minutes notice.

'Difficult DP Type 2' (Untalented/Inexperienced) is a more dangerous beast. As an Emerging Director, you are much more likely to be confronted with Type 2 than Type 1 — who is far too busy to be bothered with an unimportant film like yours. 'Difficult DP Type 2' will attempt to put the project off the rails at some point in Pre-Production. He (and it's so often a 'he') is a political creature. He will have already seen off all the competition, starting with your own list of potential Cinematographers. He'll have done that by undermining your instincts and skills and convincing your Producer that only he has the ability to bring the show in on time. The next trick is to lobby for an increase in the Camera Department's budget, by robbing other Departments of theirs. To do this, he'll pretend a knowledge of matters that are beyond his own specialty. He'll insist, for example, that the Costume or Art Departments are inflating their needs — (they probably are, but that's beside the point). Unless his protests, insinuations and downright lies are checked, the flow of cash will go towards the 'tools' he claims to need for *his* 'Look', or for additional crew members he must have for Camera. It doesn't stop there. All areas are subject to his 'superior' taste, knowledge and skill. Scenes in the script won't work — and he can get a script doctor to fix it. Particular locations aren't right — but he knows of better ones. The Make-Up Artist isn't up to the job — but, naturally, he's got the number of the right person. There's someone at a major studio who will get all the required costumes much cheaper, but she'll have to be brought on as Costume Supervisor. This turns out to be his girlfriend. The worst of these types soon appear to be more Unit Production Manager than Cinematographer, and it's hard to get them to focus on the job that you thought they were there to do. Worse, once shooting starts you will find that they see themselves more as your Co-Director than your Cinematographer. Unless you get control of the situation, don't be surprised if someone close to the Production Office whispers in your ear one day that 'Difficult DP Type 2' had lunch with the Producer and suggested that you should be replaced — by him!

How do you deal with all this? First, let me tell you that the picture I've just drawn is not fantasy. When you're starting out, the scenario of 'Difficult DP Type 2' is all too real. See it as a test of whether you've really got what it takes to become a professional Director. You may as well fight, because if you don't — if you go along with all the nonsense — the chances are the picture you make will be your last.

I've had the privilege of watching some fine Directors get rid of this problem. I recall a 'known' Indie Filmmaker being subjected to an over-inflated ego disrupting her project. Perhaps the offender thought he could get away with it because the Director was female. How wrong he was. The Director waited until the problem was becoming obvious to the Production Office. Then, in a quiet and steady voice, she turned Difficult's world upside down and put him in his place. She beautifully demonstrated the Golden Rule; *Never smack the puppy's nose until enough people have seen the mess he's making and gotten a whiff of something bad.* Then, without fuss, without anger — smack hard enough to get the puppy's attention and no more. Exert your control and move on as if nothing has happened.

But what about 'Difficult DP Type 1'? The super talented rock star? What do you do if, by some miracle of timing and budget, you have one of the finest, yet most awkward, arrogant S.O.B.s in the business on the sharp end of your camera? Simple, dear friends. You ride the wild horse. You feed the hungry beast. You subtly challenge him to give you solutions to problems that only he can solve. You make him feel that he is your mentor and guide. (And why not? he's got so much to give). You thank your Producer for bringing this genius onto the production. (He'll mention it to the rock star). To your Actors you mention how incredible it is to be guided by his brilliance. (They'll subtly protect you if the rock star becomes too obnoxious). And, once in a while, you make sure that when he's given you what *he* wants, you ask him for what *you* want — just so you can see the difference. You get through the shoot because at the end of the day (i) this D.P. might genuinely like and respect you (ii) you will have a film lit by a very talented Cinematographer, (iii) his industry-known credit will appear in close proximity to yours on the final print and, (iv) it will be so much harder for a Producer to give you a lesser talent in the future because it is now established that you only 'work with the best'.

Now that the usual caveats have been made, let's look at the positive. Like every other key creative on your team, your Cinematographer *wants* to collaborate with *you*. She will undoubtedly have strong ideas for the project and will want to listen to yours. It's worthwhile discussing those various ideas at length so that you fully understand what is being suggested, and how it will look. Your ideas and 'vision will prompt the Cinematographer to suggest particular tools, including the lighting tools, the lenses the camera support gear and various specialist items. If you don't know what a particular solution will achieve ask — or make a note to find out. Research. Discuss. Decide.

However, 'creative' is only part of the conversation with Cinematographers. There's also the not inconsiderable question of 'technical'. Which usually boils down to budget. It behooves you to have some basic understanding of 'Camera Packages', or at least be able to ask intelligent questions. Cinematographers often have a variety of cameras, suitable for different budgetary levels, that they are familiar with and prefer to use. This is handy, because familiarity with any kind of tool breeds speed, assurance, knowledge and even experimentation. Insisting on your own preferred camera and lighting packages seems counter-productive unless you have a very solid reason 'why' — and bear in mind that distribution and exhibition goals can be affected by the choice of camera, so your Producer must agree.

This is an important consideration, especially in a world of so many different formats, codecs, standards and 'delivery' criteria. If you believe that your film will be of a quality that will allow for future availability on a major streaming service — like Netflix, for example — you need to make sure that your entire production *and* post-production workflow and pipeline meets the technical requirements of that particular distributor.

Streaming services provide "approved" lists and "requirements" data. A quick look at one of those major streaming services reveals that this particular distributor currently "approves" seven manufacturers — ARRI, Canon, Panasonic, RED, Panavision, Sony and Blackmagic Design. Within the brands, certain cameras are approved by the distributor — while others don't make the list. In this instance, the C300 Mk II is one of five approved cameras from Canon. Six Panavision cameras are listed, including the Varicam 35. The ARRI Alexas are there in LF, Mini LF and 65 flavors. RED is well-represented, including 'brains' that I'd never heard of until I read the "approved" list. Then, you (or rather your producer and cinematographer) need to check the "Capture Requirements" — specific demands the distributor is making regarding issues such as capture format and compression, types of sensor. Bit rates and minimum data rates. The camera's capabilities in Color Space. Metadata. Aspect Ratio. Approvals for B-Cameras — crash, drone, underwater, etc.

Providing as much detailed information as you can in your early meetings gives the Cinematographer (i) a glimpse into how you see the story, and the audience reactions you are looking for in specific moments, (ii) an insight into the kind of 'Look' you're hoping to achieve, (iii) a significant understanding of a proposed color palette, (iv) what to expect in terms of compositional framing, (v) how much, and what kind of, camera movement might be used, (vi) the size of lighting package, including special lighting effects, required, and (vii) the type of camera and probable lenses that should be in the camera package.

Your Cinematographer needs to get into your head. Or at least, the part of your head that is filled with your 'vision' of the film. Most of all, she needs to understand the story the way you do and get an insight into how you want to reveal and inform the audience about the characters. She needs to see the locations or studios that are likely to be used. She needs to hear your preliminary thoughts on how you intend to block your actors. You have to share those 'Look' ideas you have — no matter how imprecise. And if you have ideas about an Image System (see *Decoding The Script*), you have to open up that discussion.

By the time you've been through this process, your Cinematographer will have a clear idea of how the story should be shot, how different characters may be framed and lensed, and know what lighting and support tools she'll need. She will have a good understanding of how to make the world of the film cohesive, and how the use of lenses, color, lighting and movement will follow an arc — parallel with the unfolding of the story — and subtly define the individual Acts.

Don't be shy in getting your message over. You'll be surprised at how helpful your Cinematographer will find this — and how much your thoughts and obvious commitment will energize and inspire. Your relationship is going to be a deep one. You're two brains with different skills pointed in the same direction. It's a powerful relationship when it's working well — which is why Director/Cinematographer teams are common. *Citizen Kane* without Orson Welles *and* Greg Tolland is unthinkable. David Lean without Freddie Young? Hard to imagine. Bergman without Nykvist? No, thanks. The Coens and Roger Deakins. Scorsese and Balhaus. The list is long.

That said, you will find, especially on lower-budgeted productions, that very often a Producer has no interest in a Director/Cinematographer relationship and wants to hire a particular person because that individual brings an equipment package. The Cinematographer, for example, who owns a RED camera and offers himself and his gear at an 'affordable' rate. When the deal is done, you're locked into not only a specific camera, but also a Cinematographer. The choice has been the Producer's. A choice that might work for the budget, but not necessarily for the project. Just because someone owns a camera, a grip truck, a catering company or an Avid editing suite, doesn't automatically make them the most suitable candidate. If you give up your rightful role of selection, then you've already lost a substantial part of your 'control'. You have, in effect, been given the responsibility for making the film without the authority to do so. Misery awaits unless you are very fortunate indeed — or if you simply don't care.

It may seem that by focusing so much on your relationship with the Cinematographer, I don't consider your relationship with the Production Designer/Art Director to be critical. It is. Perhaps more so. From careful reading and decoding of the script you will have brought to the project your 'vision' for the Special World of the film. This is the environment the story lives in, the architecture through which your characters move. It is the Special World that you are inviting your audience to enter.

As the Director, you don't have to know how to build that 'vision', how to physically manifest it — in fact, your 'vision' of the Special World may not be complete or be seen only dimly. It is the Production Designer who will help you conjure up the Special World, collaborating with you on *all* the visual, atmospheric and tactile aspects of the film's Special World. The Production Designer can, and should, help you zero in on how your sets and locations will materialize on film, how lighting and camera placement will affect those spaces and the Actors moving within each space, the tonal shifts of weather and season, the sense of time and period, the enhancement of the scene in terms of set dressing and practical lighting and properties, the correct selection and use of props, the correct and appropriate vehicles, animals and greenery, the overall texture, color and tonality not only of individual scenes, but how that tonality will seamlessly move throughout the film. Last, but far from least, a Production Designer will work with you on how your characters will appear — not only in terms of costume, make-up and hair but also their *physical* condition. (The characters' emotional and mental condition is your area alone).

If it's in the Frame, the Production Designer will have responsibility for it. It's a massive oversight and, sometimes a Herculean task — all done in service of your 'vision'. If you allow the collaboration, the Production Designer will help focus your thoughts, and offer suggestions not just to the practicalities of the scene under discussion but with ways to fill out and enhance your 'vision'. If you don't believe me, look at every single film that Kubrick ever made and consider the detail in each frame. Then consider the Production Designers — because although Stanley Kubrick might have been an obsessive researcher, he still needed to collaborate with Art Departments capable of meeting or exceeding his expectations. You probably haven't heard of Ken Adam, Roy Walker, Leslie Tomkins or Anton Furst. By rights, their names should be as well known to serious filmmakers as are the names of brilliant Cinematographers.

Every Hitchcock film you ever saw (and I trust it has

been many) was 'production designed' to the limit. Hitchcock, like so many of the best Directors, was meticulous — employing a discerning process of selection that began in the first moment of collaboration with his key creatives. They'd find notes specific to their craft in the margins of the script he'd send them — and from that the ideas and the collaboration would flow. It's important to realize that good Directors are seldom rigid or dictatorial in collaboration. Hitchcock, for example, would be open to all the creative interpretations, alternatives and suggestions presented for his consideration until he made his final choice or decision. That's how it works between Directors and their Creative Teams — that's why Film is a collaborative enterprise, but a Director's medium.

Back to the less-rarified world of 'low budget' production. Production Design still counts — perhaps more so, because a well-designed 'low-budget' film is going to be much more satisfying to an audience (and potentially much more successful) that a 'low-budget' film that has not been carefully designed. If, for example, you have a scene in a barn where a couple are making love during a thunderstorm, then it's the Production Designer you really need to speak to first — yes, before you speak to the Cinematographer. Everything concerning that barn — from whether it's a location that needs to be scouted and locked down or built on a sound stage — has to be envisioned. How old is it? Wooden timbers? Flaking paint? Rusting metal? Is livestock present — a horse in a stall, perhaps? Is there farm machinery? If so, what type? What vintage? Are the couple making love on a straw floor, or against a stack of grain sacks? Are the barn doors open and, if so, what is the view beyond? Is it a sunny afternoon, or a rainy night? Let's go with "a stormy night". How will the barn be lit? Hurricane lamps, or the headlights of an old truck? How hard is the rain falling outside? How violent are the lightning flashes? Is the 'feel' of the scene nostalgic, or is it there something discordant and unsettling about it? What are the principal camera angles — what areas can be left untouched by the set dresser? What state are the actors in? Have they gotten soaked in the storm? What are they wearing? If the scene is to be dimly lit, what costume color choices should be made to help them pop out of the darkness? Given that the couple are making love, is there going to be 'business' in taking off clothes, removing boots, ripping bodices, etc.? It's important to know now so the Costume Department is aware down the line.

Do you see how important this meeting has become? *Love In The Barn* is perhaps a two-minute scene which your schedule already tells you has to be shot in under four hours. You can't waste precious time on the shoot day deciding if the actor is wearing leather boots or canvas sneakers, if the parked vehicle is a truck or an old sedan, if there's a horse in the stall or hens in the background. If you and the Production Designer arrive at a very clear idea of what is required, then time is saved. Further, Art Department costs and required labor for that scene can quickly be calculated and plans made. The Production Designer will make drawings and copious notes and liaise with the Location and Costume Departments while you keep the U.P.M. and the Producer up to speed.

Once a location has been found, or a sketch made of the studio set that will be constructed, you can now meet with the Cinematographer to discuss *Love In The Barn*. It's vital that the Cinematographer sees the initial layout and understands how you will 'block' the scene. It's the Cinematographer who'll communicate to the Electrical & Lighting Department the tools required to light the barn interior (following discussion as to whether the lighting will seem to be coming from the hurricane lamps, the old truck's headlights or a new idea entirely). The Cinematographer will also figure out what is needed to 'backlight' the rain that's pouring down outside (so that the audience can actually see it) and arrange for the lightning strikes. Finally, the Cinematographer will ask about camera support — if, for example, you want motion around the Actors during the lovemaking, or some kind of dolly or crane shot. From that, the Camera and Grip Department budgets can be fine-tuned for the scene and, following discussions with the third leg of your Visual Design team — the Costume Department — you'll have a very complete Breakdown for *Love In The Barn*.

With most of the work now complete regarding (i) locations and studio sets, (ii) the lighting and camera requirements and (iii) the principal design elements in each scene, you can now return to the Costume and Make-Up & Hair Departments. While you've been away — and based on your earlier briefings regarding the overall 'Look' — they will have examined the script and the cast and come up with practical suggestions and ideas that can now be filtered down to final selections and choices. Seeing sketches, photos and fabrics — and the occasional Actor dressed in costume — can seem bewildering if this is not an area you feel confident in. Trusting the experts is important, but so too is trusting your own instinct — especially that feeling you get when something doesn't quite meet your 'vision'.

On a personal note, I find communicating with the Costume Department incredibly hard. It's not their fault, it's mine. I get called to a pre-production meeting in an office, or corner of a warehouse where the team is working, and I'm asked to look at an Actor wearing costume. (Sometimes it's photographs of the Actor in the character costume, but not always). I am then asked if I 'approve' the costume — and, of course, I have no idea. Why? Because looking at a costumed Actor in an environment that bears no resemblance to the actual space the character inhabits is something I find disorientating. I just can't picture it. Suddenly, it's not the 'dream' I'm having in my head. The costumed Actor is in front of me, but the 'Special World' of the film is not present — so the Actor looks alien and unnatural. My brain starts asking if it's because the costume is 'wrong'. Then my anxiety-flushed mind starts wondering if maybe it's the Actor who is wrong — and I've made a terrible error in casting. All the while, both Actor and Costume Department are watching my frozen reaction and assuming I'm hating what I'm seeing, Very uncomfortable for everyone. I've overcome this weakness by imagining the character buying or selecting the clothes that he or she is wearing. The answer to that

— takes me halfway to an 'approve' or a 'pass'. Then, I focus on how the costume works with the Actor's complexion and eye/hair color. That takes me into a personal comfort zone. From that point on, I can start showing some degree of approval and move onto discussing with Key Costume how the wardrobe will fit into the 'Look' of individual scenes.

Costuming, it turns out, is another area where a Producer can interfere in a 'positive' manner for the budget, but a potentially disastrous way for the film. Product placement rears its ugly head. I've worked on shows where the entire cast was costumed in clothes from the same manufacturer or fashion house with complete disregard for storyline or character definition. Directors get sullen and miserable when that kind of thing is forced upon them.

The meetings with the members of your Visual Design Team will have focused concepts for the 'Look'. The scouts you've made of probable locations and studio space now makes various forms of 'pre-visualization' — or 'Pre-Viz' — an achievable idea. With 'Pre-Viz' you can firm up those concepts and have something solid to show to your Department Heads and Producers.

Although I'm in favor of waiting until this point in the process before I start any storyboarding or 'Pre-Viz' type of work, there are many filmmakers who, by the time Pre-Production begins and meetings arranged with Cinematographers and Production Designers, have already invested heavily in time and expense in creating 'Storyboards', 'Mood Boards 'and 'Animatics'.

'Pre-Viz' runs the gamut; A quick sketch on a napkin; precisely drawn frames of shots representing an edited sequence (Storyboard); a carefully conceived and produced booklet that gives the flavor of the proposed project (Deck); full-color images of a scene illustrating tone, color palette and atmosphere (Mood Board); fully rendered sequences created with 3-D animation tools, virtual lighting, virtual camera movement, virtual environments and "voiced" virtual actors utilizing virtual props (Animatics) — and not forgetting my own favorite... scaled-down models of the set and/or location complete with miniature lamps that will replicate the intended lighting design. Go ahead and knock yourself out; for as much as you feel the need and have the time and funds.

Storyboards are ideal not only for communicating with your Cinematographer and Production Designer, but also for Stunt Coordinators, Assistant Directors, and Visual Effects Supervisors. They allow a Producer to get a glimpse of where it's going — which creates confidence. They allow a Director to work out how to shoot a sequence or, following collaboration, how to adjust shooting to get a better and more efficient result.

Mood Boards are useful to Cinematographers to help them understand a required color palette, useful to Production Designers to understand the project's texture and particularly useful to Producers when they're meeting with investors or marketing folks — which is why Mood Boards tend to be renderings made long before pre-production begins.

Models are impressive in meetings. They are helpful in judging scale and working out cast blocking, set dressing requirements and, importantly, camera angles and lighting issues.

Animatics are all of the above. They are extremely impressive and can go a long way in identifying optimum ways to light and shoot a sequence, including how the Actors will be blocked, and how the edit might look.

However, I don't care much for 'Pre-Viz' that goes into excessive detail. I know that sounds counter-intuitive, maybe even irresponsible — but, unless a sequence is extremely complex, I find that overly-detailed 'pre-viz' somehow creates a rigidity I'll do anything to avoid. Images created for storyboards and animatics have the effect of everybody thinking that is the only way to shoot the sequence. They become a dogma that must be adhered to. Perhaps it's the experience I had as a T.V. Commercials Director that makes me shudder when I see a Storyboard. In commercials, the Storyboard is more important than the Director. The Director shoots the Storyboard. I can still hear the voices of Agency Creatives saying; *'Just the 'board, thank you'*. A Director who veers "off-board" is a rogue Director. And then, when you obey all the dictums and the rigid frames of the Holy Storyboard — what happens? The Creatives sit in their screening rooms and say; *'Gee, the footage is kinda disappointing — but it looked so good on the Storyboard!'* So, I don't shoot Storyboards and I'm certainly not a slave to them. I'll use one for something tricky, to get the point across to the team or to make the Producer relax — but I'm going to use it in the same way I look at a map. The route may be clear, but if there's an interesting side-road that will take me to the same place in less time — I'm going to explore.

And now to the old caveat. I'm being repetitive, I know, but it's important for your success both now and in your future career. Keep control of your film and do not accept responsibility for *anything* without the authority to decide how it is going to be achieved. One of your primary functions as the Director is to assemble the right team for the particular film you are making. *You* are the judge of who is the right person to fill each key job in this specific and unique production — nobody else. That doesn't mean you make decisions arbitrarily or out of thin air. You ask questions, you listen to suggestions and advice, you look at show reels, you meet with prospective hires, you watch films the person under consideration has contributed to. You even make phone calls to other Directors or Producers and ask for their recommendations or for their experiences. It's your job, and you give up that responsibility at your own risk.

Allow me to cement this concept — the requirement to explore every avenue into being fully prepared.

One day, many years ago, I was hanging out in the office of a British company that had produced a film, directed by

Geoffrey Reeve, which featured an 8-minute high-speed boat chase through Amsterdam (*Puppet On A Chain,* 1971). A call came in from Steven Spielberg inquiring if he could see the film and speak to Geoffrey because he was prepping a boat chase of his own for the picture he had in pre-production (*Indiana Jones & The Last Crusade,* 1989). To know that the most famous director in the world called a small independent company about a film most people had forgotten about, made me realize how much effort serious filmmakers put into their preparation. (No doubt Mr. Spielberg also viewed boat chase footage from *Live and Let Die,* (1973) — although the time frame perhaps wasn't right for him to have seen the most mind-blowing boat chase of all time, Dick Maas' *Amersterdamned,* (1988).

Modesty forbids me from relating a similar experience of my own.... oh, well — alright, if you insist. The phone call was from the late Richard Marquand (*Return of the Jedi*, 1983) during preparation for what turned out to be his last film, (*Hearts of Fire*, 1987). My point is this. If Richard Marquand and Steven Spielberg could expend time and effort to make calls to other (relatively obscure) Directors to seek creative and technical advice — so can you.

CHAPTER SEVEN

Set Operations

Two persons and a camera can make a quality picture that gets international sales and festival distribution, (*Cavite*, 2005). A bare-bones crew with three iPhone 5s' can run around the streets of West Hollywood and make a film that premieres at Sundance and is picked up for limited theatrical distribution, (*Tangerine,*2015). With luck, judgment, persistence and a soupçon of talent, sooner or later you too may step up from the picture made with your friends on a month of weekends and find yourself responsible for directing productions with Serious Money behind them.

The more Money, the more Stars. The more Stars, the more Crew. The more Stars and Crew, the more required support systems. Drivers, personal assistants, runners, 'stand-ins', stunt 'doubles', security personnel, assistant directors, production assistants, company secretaries, production accountants, assistant editors, prosthetic makers, wig makers and hair stylists, masseurs, personal trainers, personal chefs, cast and crew caterers, armorers, historical researchers, technical consultants, riggers, stand-by painters, production office coordinators. The list is almost infinite

At a rough count, in excess of 900 people are required for a major international feature film. That's just the 'credited' personnel, behind which stand many others — agents, lawyers, managers, travel coordinators, finance facilitators, film commissioners, brand managers, publicists, marketing and sales representatives, studio and distribution executives. It takes a village to make and market a major motion picture. A very large and highly-populated village.

Experienced Producers usually have a Production Team. They have their Casting Director, their Unit Production Manager and their Assistant Director — who in turn have their 'go-to' colleagues — Location Managers, Production Coordinators, Key Wardrobe and Make-Up Persons, Transport Captains and Production Assistants. Perhaps the Producer has a favorite Cinematographer and Production Designer or won't work without a particular Editor or Composer.

While this is actually a good thing in episodic television production where multiple Directors come onto a show during its season and are simply required to maintain the pre-existing, Producer-selected elements while performing the function of Head of the Acting Department, long-term arrangements between Producers and Key Creatives can make it much more difficult to direct a feature film the way you might wish. There is a human tendency to tackle a problem using the same methodology that 'worked' in the past, or to discount a fresh idea that doesn't fit the team's ethos. If, for example, there is already a Production Designer on the team who dislikes, or disapproves of, the visual references you are bringing to the meetings, it can become difficult to fight both his taste and his lengthy relationship with the Producer.

As you progress from shoot to shoot, your ultimate goal should be to build your *own* team. There is neither time nor resources during Production and Post-Production for hit-or-miss approaches to professional services. When you surround yourself with people you can depend on creatively and technically, the more fun you start having, the faster you are able to work, and the lower your anxiety level.

In the beginning of your career, however, you may have to trust your Producers to make appropriate decisions on Crewing. Some of the people you find yourself working with might not be a 'fit' in the long-term, but you'll eventually find people you like and trust. You might think that those people who started out helping you on your student or early self-funded projects would be exactly the right people to take with you when you are given the opportunity to direct professionally and at a higher level. I know it sounds harsh, and against every 'romantic' precept, but think very, very carefully before you take friends who've helped you out on your first 'semi-pro' projects onto a production they are not experienced enough to handle. You might think; *'Hold on, what about me? I'm not fully experienced either! My friends and I worked towards this together — they deserve to get a chance'*. That might be true, but on your debut feature the Producer knows you're inexperienced, and that's why he's surrounding you with professionals. While it's entirely acceptable to recommend your friends into positions where they can gain more experience, these should not be 'Head of Department' positions unless you are confident they can do the job right. That said, there are two positions where I would urge you to *never* to hire a friend in the belief that he or she can learn on the job.

Those positions are; Unit Production Manager and First Assistant Director. An experienced U.P.M. and 1st A.D. are going to get the picture made for you — if you let them.

Some titles seem to be interchangeable. They're not, in actual fact, but confusion can arise. You will sometimes find the Unit Production Manager (a.k.a. Production Manager) referred to as the Line Producer (responsible for every 'Line Item' in the budget). But on most productions, the Line Producer oversees the U.P.M., and in turn is overseen by the Production Supervisor, the Producer and the Executive In Charge of Production. There's another role with the job title Production Coordinator which can get mistaken for U.P.M., as the work seems to be similar, but usually the Coordinator floats between Line Producer and U.P.M. and is subordinate to both.

In pre-production the U.P.M. will be concerned with almost every aspect of bringing the production into being. The principle concern will be to create the Schedule/Stripboard — relating all the decisions to the available budget and time. In fact, that is a U.P.M.s most necessary skill — the ability to look at a scene in a script and know (i) how long it will take to shoot, (ii) what equipment is likely to be needed, (iii) what crewing will likely be required, (iv) how much time will be required for set-building, set dressing, costuming, special make-up, stunt work, etc., and (v) how much of the budget needs to be set aside to shoot it. They U.P.M. will be very hands-on in terms of getting locations locked down and permitted, stages contracted, 'below-the-line' crew contracted, organizing travel and hotels, generating documentation for equipment rentals and purchases, sourcing vendors and suppliers. In short, the U.P.M. is a highly organized individual who lets nothing go to chance. They are responsible for the budget and they will know how much things are supposed to cost. They are most often people who can come up with solutions — they should be able to work with directors in such a way that 'vision' is not compromised, and challenges can be overcome. A very tough job — but if you and your U.P.M. understand and trust each other and if you respect their experience and know-how, you will be supported and championed. Simple as that. Of course, sometimes you will have to fight, and perhaps even sulk. A U.P.M. expects that and if they understand what it is you need, and the advantage and value it will bring to the project, a good one will work hard to make it happen. People often don't see the importance of a good working relationship between U.P.M. and Director — but it's a vital relationship to develop and sustain.

In the normal course of events, the Producer and the U.P.M./Line Producer will be working off-set and out of sight. You won't notice them until lunchtime — unless something unexpected and problematic happens. The 1st A.D. on the other hand, is beside you throughout the day, so it's important that you communicate well with this person.

Sometimes, you may have the misfortune to be working with people who aren't as competent as they think they are (and let's hope it's not your best friend!), which is why I made a point of warning you to go through the Breakdown and Schedule very carefully making sure that nothing is missed, and that time has been properly allotted for the work you need to do. U.P.M.s and 1st A.D.s are not mind readers — they cannot help you if you don't explain to them what you need.

There are Producers who believe that a 1st Assistant Director should be an aggressive, hard-charging drill sergeant with a loud voice. There are many sets where these types swagger and bully their way through the day. I find their technique ineffective and annoying. I prefer a quiet, calmly attentive 1st A.D. Someone who is keenly aware of the time pressure, but who keeps the crew moving forward with a request rather than a screamed obscenity. 'Screamers' tend to be incompetent and overlook the details. You need an A.D. who is very organized and very alert — people who are constantly 'present'.

There's another type of 1st AD to avoid. 'The Novice Producer's Friend'. I urged you not to bring one of your *own* friends on as 1st AD. Unfortunately, that doesn't prevent the first-time Producer from doing so. Occasionally it's the Private Investor 'Executive Producer' who insists on appointing someone he trusts to watch over how his money is spent. Neither of these parties understands how important it is to have an experienced professional in the position. They think the entire job of a 1st AD is merely a matter of shouting at the crew and keeping things moving along. In other words, a 'Screamer', and an ignorant one at that. Such a person is dangerous because he or she feels responsible to the person who gave them the job — not to the Crew or the Production.

Dangerous? Yes. In many ways. The type is self-absorbed, bungling and without empathy. They don't understand when to push — and when not to. If something isn't going right, they lash out. They create problems where none exist, they come up with time-consuming solutions that do not solve the challenge, they alienate and exhaust the crew, they take short-cuts, they turn a shoot into a boot camp, they frighten the Actors and they turn the atmosphere sour. You don't want that.

If you add another negative quality to the type, the danger can escalate dramatically. That quality is 'Fear'. Fear of not being seen as a powerful figure who can control the shoot. Fear of not pleasing the Producer. Fear of not getting the Important Shot.

You see, when it comes right down to it, a film set is a very risky place to work. Even a minor thing going wrong can result in serious injury or death. Heavy objects are suspended above people's heads. High voltage electrical equipment and cables are present. Large and heavy pieces of metal are swinging around. There are often explosive charges on set. Vehicles that have been rigged for speed or collision. Pyrotechnics. On location there are unsafe working heights. Proximity to uncontrolled roads. Taxi-ing aircraft. Barges swinging on a rising tide. Railway tracks with heavy locomotives that can't stop. Glass. Water. Sharp objects. Weapons.

I suspect most Directors have a story or two to tell of things that nearly went badly wrong. For me, it was when a speeding stunt motorcycle just missed an elderly lady who innocently crossed into its path, or the night-shoot on top of a skyscraper hotel when I almost stepped backwards into an air shaft with a 120' drop. Then there was the explosion that blew the entire crew off its feet because Paddy the Pyro Guy used too much *plastique*, or the time we noticed that the Talent was standing barefoot in water — and the water was heading towards a live distro box.

Each Department is aware of safety issues and knows the precautions to take. But the Assistant Director is the person who must ensure set safety. Everyone on the set, actors and crew, depends on the 1st A.D. to tell them if the situation is safe or not. This is why you need someone who is quietly capable of informing the entire crew, including the Producer and the Director, that the situation is dangerous, and a re-think is in order or additional care needs to be taken.

It's a job that requires 'character'. Find out the kind of 'character' your 1st A.D. has — and when you find a good 'un, don't let her go.

Finally, mention must be made of someone else that low-budget, in-a-hurry-to-get-it-done-and-save-money Producers ignore at their peril. The Script Supervisor — a position that in days of yore used to be filled by a woman who was dismissively given the title of 'Continuity Girl'. Times, and the job title, have changed. The importance of the job has not. There should really be an entire chapter devoted to their work, but I'm going to break it down to the essential take-aways from a Director's standpoint.

The Script Supervisor is your memory. No, not just of what happened in the immediate past while (s)he was making copious notes and a log regarding the last shot. If you are able to bring your Script Supervisor into Pre-Production early enough, then they are your memory of the decisions you arrived at before Principal Photography began. It's easy for a Director, especially under pressure, to forget some detail vital to maintain continuity or to prevent what might become a problem in post-production. One part of the Script Supervisor's job is to remind a Director of that detail (and sometimes to explain why the decision had been made in the first place). They can't do that if they haven't had an insight into Pre-Production planning, been able to pick your brain as to the 'whys' and 'hows' or had time to go through the script and the Breakdowns with the proverbial tooth-comb.

The second function of the Script Supervisor is to be, in effect, the first person in the Post-Production Department to see the film. It's like having a keen-eyed, detail-orientated Picture and Dialogue Editor standing beside you all day. Now, some Directors, Actors and Key Creatives get uncomfortable and irritable with this, because a good Script Supervisor will draw attention to anything that is incorrect. Some examples? A wrong 'eyeline'. An Actor with his shirt tucked in, when it should be untucked. A line of dialogue missing. A word mispronounced. An Actress with her hair falling across her face, when it should be brushed behind her ear. A prop that has been put in the wrong place. A reverse matching shot where the wrong focal length lens is being used. Shots that may not cut together in the edit room. An action or line that makes no sense in terms of 'Story'. Shots composed in ways where the spatial geometry will confuse the audience. Previously unnoticed artwork on a wall, a t-shirt or a 'fridge door that hasn't been licensed.

The number and variety of things that a Script Supervisor might draw everyone's attention to is vast — and nobody likes to be told they're doing something wrong. Some people like it even less with they're being told so by a woman — and the majority of Script Supervisors are, to this day, female.

Naturally, due to age and my acceptance of any job on a film set that happens to be going, I have fulfilled the task myself — and, let me tell you, it's very tough to stand your ground (in the midst of an exhausted Crew) and tell a Director and a Cinematographer that the previous shot needs to be done again due to a technical error that neither they nor anyone else has noticed or seems to care about.

In summary:

A good U.P.M. will take care of your crew, give you space to work and put out the fires that will inevitably arise — including those started by the disenchanted crew-member who wants to start a mutiny (and most shoots have one).

A good 1st A.D. will keep your film moving forward at the right speed, make sure you have everything available to you when you need it, and will keep everyone both calm and on their toes.

A good Script Supervisor will keep your shooting on the straight and narrow, then send all the historical data into Post Production so that the inevitable questions as to 'where', who' and 'why' can be answered without fuss or panic.

With these three positions covered by experienced, good-natured professionals you should be able to overcome any challenge that arises and work with focus and efficiency.

CHAPTER EIGHT

Finding Balance

    Productive and enjoyable relationships between Director and Producer, Director and Crew and Director and Cast are built on mutual respect. When you think about it, what would cause you, a Director, to respect those people who are working as your colleagues and partners in your creative effort? It boils down to this; respect lies in knowing you can trust them to understand what they are doing, and to do it skillfully — or to have a workable solution for any challenge that arises, no matter what aspect of their craft that involves, and no matter how difficult. Producer, Cast and Crew have no less expectation of you, dear Director. They need to know that you are clear as to what you're doing, that you are doing it with an efficiency and thoughtfulness that exceeds their expectations, and that — no matter what happens — you can steer the project in the direction it's supposed to be going without wasting Time, Money or Energy.

    This chapter is not an inventory of what do in specific circumstances — there are far too many variables in film production to make that possible. Rather, this chapter seeks to present you with a *balanced* mindset that allows for good solutions to all your technical and creative challenges. And that mindset begins in Pre-Production. Over and over, I see Directors lose the respect of their Producers and their Crews (and often their Casts) because they are not fully prepared to solve a particular problem, and their reaction is to stand firm on a bad solution. I've noticed that Directors with this lack of flexibility tend to be either (i) under-prepared or over-prepared — *and* — either (ii) under-resourced or over-resourced — but whichever of these polarities or combinations they land on, the result is always the same and it is identical. Money is wasted. Time is squandered. Energy is spent.

What do I mean by this paradoxical view that different preparation and resource levels lead to the same result? Allow me one of my crasser analogies so that I can present the concept.

Most obviously, and egregiously, I'm thinking of the kind of Director, often abetted by an over-optimistic Cinematographer, who brings a tool onto the set that is far too complex, and too powerful, for the job it is required to do and ends up pushing the creative team into taking an approach that is too ambitious for the Director's skillset. Let's call this Director — Alpha Guy. He's certainly over-resourced. Whether he's under-prepared or over-prepared is equally dangerous — as we will see.

Alpha Guy's opposite — Beta Boy — is also frequently spotted amongst the natural fauna of the world's film sets. Beta Boy doesn't request the big artillery for his shoot. Usually, that's because he doesn't have much knowledge of the larger pieces of film-making weaponry available to him, but more often it's because his Producer has made it clear that using the big guns is not within the budget. You'd think that a low budget Director would be under-prepared when compared to a production operating at a higher level. But sometimes Beta Boy is surprisingly over-prepared — which brings its own set of unfortunate consequences — as we will learn.

SELECTING FOR SUCCESS | 117

What Alpha Guy and Beta Boy have in common is this. They haven't approached their Pre-Production process by asking themselves three important questions. In the case of both Alpha Guy and his low budget cousin, Beta Boy, those questions might have been;

- *What equipment or technique do I need to utilize to achieve the result I'm looking for?*
- *How many different approaches can I take to achieve that result and how effective will each approach be in telling the story?*
- *What will different approaches, techniques and tools cost me in terms of Time, Money and Energy?*

Alpha Guy networks with friends and colleagues who are, at this moment, higher on the production food chain than he is. A Director he admires has just used a Techno Crane on her latest shoot and has waxed poetic about it ever since. The Techno Crane is a telescoping crane with an extending jib arm, capable of 360° rotation and a telescoping speed of up to 7 feet per second. The remote head can be under-slung for ultra-lo-angle shots, or over-slung for added height. Chapman Leonard's version, the Hydrascope, has a remote head that is equally at home under water — which is super exciting. The most popular versions extend to a useful 32'. There's even a Super-Techno 100 which claims — you've guessed it; 100' of elevation. A Techno Crane offers very smooth and almost silent movement. It's incredibly maneuverable and fast to set-up — but requires two trained operators, minimum. In short, this is one sweet piece of equipment. So much so, it has become a symbol to Alpha Guy. A symbol of his standing and importance. He is determined to bring one onto his shoot.

Beta Boy is aware of the Techno Crane and would love to have one on his shoot to "elevate" his production value, but his Producer has never heard of a Tech-what? and couldn't afford it in any case. When told that it's a type of jib crane, the producer suggests a Jimmy Jib, which — again — is a very useful, but much less expensive, piece of equipment. A Jimmy Jib comes in flavors from 13' to 40' in terms of 'reach' and also has a remote head. One man can operate it, with set-up taking about an hour. Beta Boy shrugs his shoulders, considers if he should indulge in a brief moment of passive-aggression to get something more exciting than a Jimmy Jib, and decides it's not a fight worth making.

Both these Directors think they're going to get a lot of use out of their respective 'tools'. Beta Boy's been told he can have his Jimmy Jib for two days, and Alpha Guy's got the Techno Crane for five days if he wants it. Both went into this knowing that there was one particular sequence that could use a crane — but now that the equipment request has been green-lighted they take another look at their scripts to see if there are additional scenes where the super-sexy gear can be used. The 'Setting-Up-For-Failure' has begun, my friends.

But first, let's look at the scene(s) that inspired their original thoughts to use a crane of some sort. A sequence where four separate actions are taking place simultaneously within one large location. Something like this;

45. EXT. OFFICE & WAREHOUSE — DAY

BIG FRANK leaves the front office and stops to light a cigarette. LITTLE TONY is washing the BMW.

              BIG FRANK
       You not done yet, Tony?

             LITTLE TONY
       Sorry, Frank.

46. INT. TALL BUILDING OPPOSITE — CONTINUOUS

MARVIN, at the open window on the top floor, watches BIG FRANK through binoculars — then speaks into his headset.

                    MARVIN
            He's outside.

THE STREET BELOW —

The WHITE TRUCK pulls away from a parking space.

                    BILLIE (O.S.)
                    (futzed: w/t)
            We're moving.

47. EXT. OFFICE & WAREHOUSE - CONTINUOUS

BIG FRANK inspects the BMW.

                    BIG FRANK
            Hey, ya missed a bit here, Tony.

                    LITTLE TONY
            Sorry, Frank.

IN THE STREET —

The WHITE TRUCK approaches Big Frank's Yard.

48. EXT. REAR LOADING AREA — CONTINUOUS

FRANK's CREW load the trailer. CARLOS and JACK run up the ramp and are spotted. Gunfire erupts.

49. EXT. OFFICE & WAREHOUSE — CONTINUOUS

BIG FRANK hears the gunfire…

                    BIG FRANK
            What the..?

ANGLE ON —

```
The WHITE TRUCK roars into the yard, and slews to a
stop. RAY and BILLIE jump out, guns drawn.

BACK TO SCENE —

BIG FRANK turns in confusion and panic, and finds
LITTLE TONY holding a shotgun on him…

                    BIG FRANK (CONT'D)
          Tony? Jesus! No!

                    LITTLE TONY
          Sorry, Frank.

The shotgun blast lifts BIG FRANK off his feet and
flings him across the BMW in a spray of blood.
```

    There are all kinds of pre-production business to consider in this short sequence, not least finding a location that manages to tie the various scenes into one area. For Beta Boy, this sequence is the big 'action' moment in his film — so it's natural to want to have significant tools available. For Alpha Guy, it's also a big moment in his film — but more likely one of many given that his budget is considerably higher. His pressure is to make the sequence thrilling, unforgettable and 'masterly'.

    Alpha Guy has opted for a Techno Crane and it's easy to see why he thinks that might be a good idea. With careful choreography, he could capture the entire sequence in a single shot — irrespective of the fact that there are four main areas spread out within the location — these being; (i) the area at the front of the office building where the BMW is parked, (ii) the loading area at the rear of the office building (iii) the top floor, open window interior in the five storey building opposite Frank's yard and (iv) the street leading to the yard along which comes the White Truck.

    The crane movement that Alpha Guy envisions might be something like this;

SELECTING FOR SUCCESS | 121

Sc. 45. SHOT BEGINS in a loose, MEDIUM frame that TRUCKS backwards "above" Big Frank as he leaves the office, and which slowly descends into a LO-ANGLE CLOSE-UP of Little Tony crouched down washing the front tire of the BMW. (And if you really want to get tricky, simultaneously seeing Big Frank's reflection in the shiny hubcap as he approaches the car).

RISING seamlessly into a TOP SHOT that leaves Big Frank and Little Tony far below us and takes us into the Sc. 46 part of the sequence. The shot swinging up to find MARVIN at the top floor window, and TELESCOPING at speed into a CLOSE-UP on those binoculars, then turning 180° to DE-SCEND and PAN as the WHITE TRUCK leaves it's parking space.

Continuing to DESCEND rapidly, keeping the moving White Truck first in LONG SHOT then into a LO-ANGLE shot just above street level before PANNING and moving at speed towards BIG FRANK as he inspects the car, then lifting to shoulder height and slowing to circle the car with Frank before... LIFTING up and over the roof of the office building and dropping down at the rear to find (Sc. 48) JACK and CARLOS running up the ramp, as the gun battle begins, then...

TELESCOPING at 7 feet/sec down the alley alongside the office building into a CLOSE UP of BIG FRANK as the WHITE TRUCK appears... CIRCLING round to see LITTLE TONY lift the shotgun, and SWISH PANNING back to see BIG FRANK hit and the blood squibs spray as the Wire-Pull jerks him over the BMW's hood... the sequence ENDING as the shot LIFTS UP into a BIRD'S EYE view of the scene, with Big Frank in the center of frame.

Whew. Alpha Guy has worked all this out in his head, on his storyboards, in consultation with his Cinematographer, the Stunt Coordinator and his Assistant Director. Excitement and confidence are running high. A single incredible shot is going to cover the entire sequence in ways that will astonish the audience — and affirm Alpha Guy's place as an important emerging filmmaker.

Meanwhile, Beta Boy is working on something more modest. His Shot List is broken into many separate set-ups, but each one uses the Jimmy Jib to give 'production value' to the scene(s). Maybe he starts on that hubcap reflection to see Big Frank leave his office, and then he might swing the camera over the BMW's roof establishing Little Tony at work. Perhaps he'll place Marvin not in the 5th floor window, but a 2nd floor window, and use the jib to crawl 6 or 8 feet up the brickwork until Marvin comes into shot — making it appear (with the addition of an Establishing Shot) that Marvin is on the top floor. He could then use the jib at chest height for a 2-SHOT of Ray and Billie inside the White Truck receiving the message from Marvin, then crane up into a Wide Shot to watch as the White Truck pulls away from the curb and heads towards Big Frank's yard. The gunfight scene on the loading ramp could be shot with panache using the jib for a couple of shots, varying the lens height to increase drama. And the final scene with Big Frank's assassination could end much as Alpha Guy's does with that TOP SHOT over Frank's dead body.

But.

By now you'll be aware of the big problem. Time. Alpha Guy is 'over-resourced'. He's got a significant toy to play with, so it seems wasteful and foolish not to use it for maximum effect. His plan has been properly prepared, inasmuch as he can clearly see it in his head, he's got the storyboards to prove it, and he's worked out the details with his Department Heads. Or has he? Because there's a Department Head who hasn't been consulted. And that would be the Editor. This oversight has, in fact, left Alpha Guy 'under-prepared'. He just doesn't know it yet.

Beta Boy might be 'under-resourced' in the view of many filmmakers, but he's going make the best of what he's got. He has planned his various shots in great detail, intending to use the Jimmy Jib in every set-up. He doesn't have the camera/cast choreography issues that Alpha Guy faces, but he does have a Time problem due to moving equipment and resetting for every scene in the sequence. He's aware of the Time cost, but he believes he's compensated by making his Shot List detailed and specific. He has explained everything to his Department Heads, including the Editor, and been given an enthusiastic thumbs-up from all concerned. What could go wrong? On the face of it — nothing at all. Unless Beta Boy has an attitude and a mind-set that doesn't allow him to see that he might be 'over-prepared' or that being 'under-resourced' has given him inadequate equipment for some of the shots he's got planned.

Incidentally, which of these two directorial positions appeals to you most? Not an idle question. You might be intrigued and excited by Alpha Guy's Techno Crane and the possibilities it brings — along with the implication that he has a substantial budget and a highly professional crew. Or you might be the kind of Director who prefers the creative challenge of making something great from minimal resources. The answer to that question may speak to where and how you should position your career.

In a perfect world, all might go wonderfully for both Alpha Guy and Beta Boy —but we wouldn't learn anything from that, would we? Let's stay with imperfect.

Alpha Guy spends several hours choreographing and rehearsing his shot. The afternoon is already well-advanced by the time everything is fully in place. The Cinematographer has become increasingly anxious in the past two hours, knowing that the sun is going to dip down behind some tall buildings in the distance. He's called up more lighting because he anticipates that a substantial part of the location will go into shadow. Placing the lighting takes time… and now it's the Director who is getting anxious. Finally, they get the first shot off… but that

180° turn from Marvin at the high window goes completely wrong because, as the camera turns to begin its descent towards the White Truck, there's a massive, and unwanted, lens flare. The sun has moved west and is lower than anticipated. A quick reappraisal is made. Instead of the 180° turn, the camera will now pull back, still on Marvin at the window, then drop fast to catch the moving White Truck. The lens will never make that westward turn towards the truck until it's low enough to avoid the flare. Take #2. All seems to be going great. The pull back from Marvin is better than the original plan. Then the camera descends and turns towards the White Truck — superb! No lens flare! It looks amazing in the monitors. The camera sweeps over Little Tony and Big Frank at the BMW. It's breathtaking to watch the shot go over the roof and drop down to see Jack and Carlos run up the ramp… until Jack drops his gun… and as he scrambles to pick it up Carlos collides with him… and the guys playing Frank's Crew stop their action and look around wondering what's gone wrong… and… CUT! CUT! CUT! It is now late afternoon. The sun is low in the sky, starting to send that magical golden glow across the location. The Musco Light™ is sparked and the areas in shadow become daylight again… albeit as artificial as a Monday Night Football Stadium and with the sky beyond seeming black in contrast. Alpha Guy is sweating. The Cinematographer tells him that it will be okay once they get into post-production and fix it, but there's only enough daylight left to do one more take. This will be it. The last chance. Take #3. Everyone holds their breath. Then — there it is. Complete. Big Frank, properly squibbed and bloodied, lies in center of frame in the BIRD'S EYE view that exactly matches the storyboard's final frame. The shot, encompassing 4 separate scenes, has lasted a tense 3 minutes and 18 seconds. It is perfect! Perfect! Cast and Crew start to applaud. Backs are slapped. Spontaneous hugging breaks out. What a wonderful shot!

Beta Boy's shoot is more prosaic. This is an important sequence for him, and he approaches it with care. He starts with Marvin at that 2nd storey window, crawling the camera up the brickwork. Unfortunately, the Jimmy Jib can't extend quite far enough so the hot-head has to tilt up the last few feet for the camera to see Marvin. It's not great — Marvin's head looks disembodied — so Beta Boy decides to do the same thing using a 1st floor window. He ends up with Marvin framed exactly how he wanted him, but it has taken much longer than expected. The Producer is already wondering why the 2nd floor window shot wasn't acceptable. It seems laughable to have used the crane to travel upwards a mere four feet from the ground. Beta Boy's shot list now demands the ESTABLISHING shot of the building, and then a REVERSE from the top floor for Marvin's POV of the White Truck. At this point, nobody's questioning Beta Boy's shot order, but Time is eating away. Back on the street, they re-park the White Truck and set up a side shot into the truck interior to see BILLIE and RAY — a shot of an action not mentioned in the script, but which the Director feels is important to fully 'cover' the scene. Much time is taken getting the jib stable and under control and timing the swing and rise movement for Billie's dialogue line (an off-screen line in the script!) and the truck drive-off. Once again, the Producer is wondering why a similar shot couldn't have been made in half the time, using sticks. Some of the crew are beginning to wonder the same thing. They move down the street to the entrance to the yard, where Beta Boy sets up the REVERSE, placing the Jimmy Jib in Big Frank's yard and rehearsing a shot that will start at ground level in the street with the White Truck driving towards camera and rising up as it makes its turn into the yard, revealing Big Frank, Little Tony and the BMW. It takes an inordinate amount of time. The Producer and Assistant Director are becoming increasingly concerned. Beta Boy moves, logically, further into the location and starts to shoot Sc. 65 where Big Frank steps out of the office and is seen reflected in the BMW's hub cap. Lunch is called. The Producer takes his Director aside and expresses the Time Concern. Beta Boy explains that everything is going to be okay. But around mid-afternoon, everything is not okay. Beta Boy has stuck rigidly to his Shot List and it's become clear to everyone that he's shooting details in ways that barely make sense. He uses the Jimmy Jib on a track to do a LO-ANGLE shot under the BMW to reveal where Little Tony has hidden his shotgun, and then lifted up 3 feet into a frame where Little Tony is seen reflected in a wing mirror. The A.D. has quietly asked if some shots are really necessary and Beta Boy, fully committed to the edit he sees in his head and the Shot List he has discussed with his Editor, isn't listening. With just 45 minutes left to shoot, they move to the rear of the building and the loading ramp. Carlos and Jack are ready. Frank's Crew know exactly what they are to do. The Prop Master/Armorer passes out the rubber submachine guns and demonstrates how to simulate recoil. Meanwhile, Beta Boy is setting the crane and rehearsing the first move. The Cinematographer quietly asks if the Director would like to shoot the scene hand-held — it would be quicker, he'd get more shots, it would add energy — but Beta Boy says 'no'. In the final minutes, with a tired crew and with actors who've been waiting all day for this scene, he is able to get four shots, all from the same position but with different jib moves. The A.D. calls it a 'wrap'. The Producer asks his Director if he got the coverage he needed. Beta Boy beams. Yes. He shot his entire List. He has every single shot he wanted. The Producer, relieved, pats the Director on the back. Everyone goes home thinking they did a good day's work — but not everyone, including the Cinematographer, thinks it was a *great* day's work.

On the face of it, all seems to have gone right for Alpha Guy and Beta Boy. But this is not so. *Then where did it go wrong?* you ask. *They got their shots, didn't they?* I agree. They got their shots. They appear to have overcome the challenges they faced. But remember, the proof is in the footage — and we haven't seen that yet, have we? In film production we have to trust that Directors have planned the work properly, given their resources, so that the material is fit for the 'edit'.

- *What we observe in production is only a small part of the complete filmmaking process.*

I know these examples appear to discuss Production, but they are actually an insight into how a Director can make a mistake in Pre-Production. I repeat. For both Directors it didn't go wrong in Production but in *Pre-Production.* Watching Alpha Guy and Beta Boy's direction on the set in these examples is akin to witnessing the last few seconds of a car wreck. The *cause* of the wreck came earlier. We are only able to fully see the *result* when the wreck is towed into the body shop that is a post-production edit suite and examined.

In Alpha Guy's case, that post-mortem examination showed that his spectacular shot, while perfectly framed and executed, lay lie a dead fish in the edit room. A sequence that on paper lasted under two pages and which should have translated to about 90 to 120 seconds on screen, now lasts a tediously uninterrupted 3 minutes and 18 seconds. It looks pretty, but there is no way for the Editor to make it less boring. Once inserted into the film as a whole, it becomes obvious that the single shot sequence, despite its clever elegance, kills the entire momentum of the story. Alpha Guy's motivation for using the Techno Crane sprang from ego and ambition, so he was unable to think it through. He spent his Pre-Production on acquiring the tool and preparing to use it. By ignoring how his footage would look in the edit room, by not having a 'vision' which he could discuss with the Editor, by accepting that the exciting storyboard frames of single moments of action would translate thrillingly into the continuous action of projected film — he left himself unprepared.

The expensive tool that his massive resources allowed him, and all the neat trickery the tool opened up for him, led him to prepare something that was likely to fail onscreen. He locked himself into a single shot, risking everything because his ego and ambition told him to go for it, and his confidence in the tool left him unprepared for the reality of the edit.

Beta Boy fared slightly better. He at least had a variety of shots to string together in his edit, which kept the sequence moving along. True, he was under-resourced, and that cost him time, and introduced some distracting shakiness into several of the shots. For many of his set-ups he'd have been far better served to have put his camera on sticks, or into the hands of an experienced operator. That would have saved time and produced better results. But his real mistake lay in over-preparing his Shot List, sticking to it despite it being obvious on-set that it wasn't working all the time, and getting carried away with the idea of using his Jimmy Jib exclusively. No doubt he told himself that crane movement in each shot would produce an immersive and cinematic experience. But the editorial reality turned out to be that the shots joined up in strange ways and the viewer's attention kept being drawn away from story and onscreen action into the camera movement itself.

So, what am I trying to tell you? Only that you have to take a step back in Pre-Production and ask yourself what your resources will allow you to do, and how those resources will affect the way you tell the story. It's acceptable to be ambitious, and equally acceptable to take on the creative challenge of minimal resources. But there has to be realism in your preparation. You have to work out where the weakness of your approach lies and be ready to take an alternative route if necessary. You have to find a balance between 'vision', time and resources. Similarly, you have to strike a good balance between proper planning and becoming so burdened with your preparation that your direction becomes rigid and inflexible and you are unable to roll with a punch or accept the serendipity of the moment.

The more technology evolves, the more possibilities are opened up for thrilling, creative shots. But with that evolution comes the temptation to place confidence in the technology rather than in your own 'vision' — and forget, or dismiss, the possibility that what the neat equipment is really doing is leading you, unsuspecting, into a quagmire.

To be honest, I don't think any director who'd been given the resources of Alpha Guy would have made the mistake of not factoring in the problem of editorial compression and finding ways to lose long, boring bits if that became a problem — but it has happened, particularly when directors are given motion stabilizers like a Steadicam™.

There have been tears and groans of disappointment too numerous to mention in edit rooms over the years when such discoveries are made, and Directors face the awful truth that their 'amazing' tracking shot fails to compare with the granddaddy of them all — Orson Welles' *Touch of Evil*, (1958).

Mostly, however, in highly choreographed shots, it's the amount of physical time required to set up, rehearse and shoot that causes the problem and forces the director to have a 'Plan B'. If you're smart, that can be compensated for on set — provided you've actually got 'Plan B'.

I imagine even gifted directors like Joe Wright can have an anxious moment — the superbly choreographed continuous shot of the Dunkirk beach scene that made it into *Atonement* (2007) was the third take before the sun went down over the horizon. There would have been insufficient light for a fourth.

CHAPTER NINE

The Art Department

I mentioned the work of the Production Designer/Art Director in 'The Look' but it deserves some further discussion. People tend to forget how important the Art Department is. It doesn't appear to be as challenging and responsible as, say, the Camera and Electrical Departments. A guy operating a $200,000 camera seems a lot more important than someone in a torn T-shirt holding a paint brush. But the lady with the paint brush is likely making a more definitive creative contribution to your picture.

Interestingly, Production Design is an area that many Producers have very little knowledge of — and this often translates into them being quite meek and accepting when the budget requirements are mentioned. They expect it's going to be expensive and, by golly, their expectations always turn out to be met! As a former Production Designer who considered a 900% mark-up on construction materials to be 'normal course of business', I can assure you that Production Design is the career to be in if you'd like to buy that second vacation home. All joking aside, Production Design in capable creative hands can give you a big bang for the buck, which makes discussion of your role in working closely with the Art Department during Pre-Production of some importance.

Nothing kills your ambitious production day quicker than an Art Department that has not got something right or has not been able to finish 99.9% of their work by the time Lights and Cameras are brought onto your set or location. A production will stop dead in the water while the Art Department frantically tries to complete a task, search for a missing element, or find a work-around for an unworkable concept. Well, maybe a few things. Like an accident, a power outage or the non-appearance of the Star — but, generally, when shooting gets held up for a considerable length of time, it's usually the Art Department at fault — although we traditionally try to pass the blame onto the Sound Department. Which is why, when a production stalls, and the crew is hanging around aimlessly, you can usually hear the Production Sound Mixer announce with quiet satisfaction, '*Not waiting for Sound*....' and it's why you have to make sure that your Art Director is both competent and has fully understood what is required.

Remember also that the Art Department has much more preparation to do in Pre-Production than anyone else, with the possible exception of Costume or Prosthetic Fabrication. It is vital to keep on top of their progress and be able to approve or adjust the work they're doing. There's nothing worse than being on-set and finding the important prop is not-quite-right, a wall needs to be repainted or a door is in the wrong place. The work is in the details. Good Art Departments are going to bring the details, the back-up details, and the back-up to the back-up. Good directors, similarly, will have suitable visual or written reference to hand to the Art Department and will make themselves available to the Production Designer and her team. Good directors will also be capable of making a choice, or at minimum, narrowing the choices down. It's true that sometimes you can't decide — on a tone, a fabric, a design, a texture, or a style. Sometimes you have to put the 'detail' in front of the camera in the correct lighting condition before you know for sure. That's okay. But you have to allow for that in both time and budget.

To help you grasp this more completely, here's a selection of actual real-life Production Design moments that could have been avoided.

Indecision: The Director couldn't decide the exact color shade required for the set. The paint crew went into overtime while they awaited his decision. Eventually, at 4 a.m., a mere three hours prior to Call Time, word came down and painting began. At 9.00 a.m., the Star came out of wardrobe and wandered onto the set. He didn't notice the *'Keep Off, Wet Paint'* notices, so he managed to get paint on his costume. There was no back-up costume. The Art Department was blamed for not making the paint dry quicker. Nobody suggested that the Director might have come to a decision earlier.

Unavailability: After four 20-hour days, the construction crew completed the set, with an hour to go before Call Time. They went to sleep in the Green Room. When the Director arrived, it was the first time he'd been to the studio. Although the set had been built according to an approved plan, and the Director had been given a scale model of the set, he and the Cinematographer decided the set wasn't tall enough for one of their shots. The construction crew were woken up to build the set 4' higher. Shooting was delayed for five hours. The Director complained to the Producer about the inadequacy of the Art Department. Nobody blamed the Director for not appearing during the 'build', nor for failing to work out earlier that his lo-angle shot required a set that was 4' higher. Nor did anyone suggest that he and his Cinematographer might have made a lens change or adjusted a camera placement to allow for a 16' high set, rather than waste five hours building it higher.

Ignorance: And then there was the Director who hadn't paid any attention to the budget limitation placed on the Art Department. He was coupled with the Producer who was too afraid to tell him. The Director wanted an actual 1950s Airstream Trailer for an Interior Night scene, a vintage Rolls Royce Silver Cloud for a car 'interior', and an authentic Dust-Bowl era Revival Meeting Tent with seating for 200 extras. The Producer had allocated a total of $2,000 for the three scenes which he had regarded as mere inserts using mock-up sets. When suggestions were made as to how to accomplish the brief, (such as doing a mock-up of the trailer interior or containing the Revival Tent scene to a 20-seat section), the Director angrily announced that he didn't want the Art Department to be *'creative'*, he wanted the real thing otherwise the audience would *'smell that it's not authentic'*. While the Assistant Art Director suppressed a smile at the mention of the word 'authentic', the Production Designer gazed helplessly at the Director's little hissy dance and wished to be on another production, in a galaxy far, far away.

Previously, in 'The Look', I offered some insight into the importance of Production Design and how it unifies your film, but it's a topic that tends to be misunderstood. Film production involves the activities of a great many disparate skills, each one having its own 'expert' requirements. We live in a world of specialization and that has led us to create 'Departments'. Your job is to control and guide those various activities, and to get the 'Departments' speaking to each other and coordinating their activities. Now I say that's your job, but often we look to the Production Designer to do a substantial part of that work (which is why it's a more important and meaningful 'credit' than Art Director').

On lower budget productions, it's not uncommon to find that 'Production Design' merely means instructing the Art Director on how the sets should look, and what props are required. But Production Design encompasses much more than that. In the serendipity that occurs almost daily for me, I found myself watching an old John Wayne movie this afternoon. (*Rio Bravo,* Warner Bros. 1959*)*. It's a Technicolor picture starring Wayne, Dean Martin and Angie Dickinson. Howard Hawks produced and directed. Art Director Leo K. Kuter. So, an 'A' list picture of its day. You might want to watch this movie. The storyline is unimportant, the action slow, the performances not especially remarkable. The most interesting thing for film buffs is Dimitri Tiomkin's score. (It included a theme which Sergio Leone referenced for *A Fistful of Dollars.*)

Why do I ask you to watch this solid, but uneventful movie? Because the Production Design is *perfectly unified*. From the Hair & Make-up Department, to Costumes, the Paint shop, the color graders at Technicolor (no mention in the credits who the color consultant was), the Art Department's prop buyers. Everything. I don't know whether it was Hawks or Kuter who was responsible, (my money is on Hawks), but everybody got the memo. Everybody. Each frame of Rio *Bravo* had been carefully controlled — a remarkable exercise in inter-departmental communication.

Take any scene at random. A Night Interior in the hotel bar. A long dialogue scene between Dickinson and Wayne. Everything in the frame — (i) the set (ii) the props (iii) the practical lighting (iv) Dickinson's hair color (v) Dickinson's mustard yellow blouse (vi) Wayne's dark beige shirt (vii) Dickinson's make-up and lip color (viii) Wayne's 'natural' make-up (ix) the overall lighting scheme — all carefully chosen so that there was complete tonal harmony in the frame. The result? The actors are very present in the scene. They're almost 3-dimensional. They are the absolute focus of our attention.

'*But*', you cry, '*movies aren't like that anymore!*' Actually, they are. Good ones that is. Films that have been made with care. They've moved on, of course, exploring other means, introducing new ideas, utilizing new techniques.

My point is this — and I only ask you to consider it, even if you're working in 'micro-ultra-low-budget' circumstances without many resources — get everybody on the same page. It's no good just 'accepting' whatever comes along. If, for example, you have a location that has a particular tonal or textural quality, then that space becomes the canvas which you will populate with costumed Actors, props, lighting and everything else that enters your frame. Achieving unity, and keeping the focus where you want it, might require tremendous thought and preparation. You could be in a meeting with the Costume Department, asking that a character be dressed so as to work best within the location and the lighting. Only to be told that this is impossible due to continuity. So, now you might have to reverse engineer previous scenes to get the Actor into the required costume — or you will have to take the costume as 'fixed' and change another element in the proposed location — the color of a wall, or the way a scene is going to be lit.

It may start to get exhausting but what you can't do is shrug your shoulders and say 'forgetaboutit'. You can't drop the tight like that. Yes, there are people who will think you crazy, or difficult. But directing a movie isn't a popularity contest. If you don't take care now — then when? In Post-Production?

Don't make me laugh.

CHAPTER TEN

Stunts

For some 'Action-Adventure' Directors, the choice of Stunt Coordinator is so vital they will delay their production until the person they want becomes available, and their Shooting Scripts are built with the knowledge that a particular Stunt Coordinator will be in charge.

Even if your goals are more modest, remember this; if an Actor jumps from the tailgate of a parked pick-up truck — it's a stunt. If an Actor has to slap another Actor — it's a stunt. If an Actor crouches down and his knee touches the ground while he fires his pistol — it's a stunt. Your Producer may tell you this is not the case. You may need to remind him that you are *both* liable for any accidents on set. And so is the 1st Assistant Director, by the way.

Even so, you will encounter pushback. Many Actors have been trained to handle minor 'stunts' or are experienced enough to know exactly what to do. Some are eager to show off those skills and they are often encouraged to do so. There are Producers who feel that something 'easy' like a simple fall, or a punch, doesn't require the expensive services of a Stunt or Fight Coordinator. So, let me belabor the point. I'd rather lose the 'fall' or the 'punch' than not have a Stunt Coordinator on set, irrespective of whether it's a Union or Non-Union production. A Director's responsibility is the safety of the Actors and Crew, and, as mentioned previously, a good 1st A.D. won't allow any foolishness.

As with every other Department Head, in the selection process you'll be guided by recommendations and you'll read resumes. You'll watch demo reels and meet potential candidates. During these 'selection' meetings, the potential Stunt Coordinator will arrive having read the script — or those portions relating to stunt work — and throw out some ideas. Your job is to decide if the proposals are going to work, enhance the project and compliment your 'vision'. The Producer's job is to figure out if those proposals are affordable.

Once the Stunt Coordinator is on the team, you'll be getting feedback on the plans being made, the training required, and the equipment needed. You should be asking questions about the amount of time you'll need to shoot the stunt. Stunt Coordinators will give you an accurate estimate, a better estimate than anyone else will give you. Incidentally, if you've been presented with a Stunt Coordinator who isn't talking about safety equipment, you might want to ask why and find out more about him and how he's regarded in the 'Stunt' community.

I mentioned training. A simple 'punch-block-punch' fight sequence can be worked out with your Actors on the day. Anything more complex will require some training and rehearsal. When the Stunt Coordinator is ready to show you the sequence (either with Stunt Performers or with the actual Actors) try to take the Cinematographer with you to observe. Stunt Coordinators are enthusiastic experts, and you're going to find that they've already worked up ways to enhance your scene and take it way beyond what you originally imagined. With your Cinematographer present, you can discuss camera placement and movement — and be fully ready on the day of the shoot to work speedily and safely.

In common with many Directors, you may not know where to place the camera to capture the 'decisive moment' of the action, the specific angle that helps "sell" the stunt without revealing its inherent 'fakery'. Don't let your ego get in the way of Asking the Expert. Coordinators respond positively to people who actually listen to their suggestions. By the same token, you needn't feel obliged to accept the first solution put forward. If your Coordinator is any good there will always be another way to achieve a workable result. Be aware that anything worked out in Pre-Production is going to save Time and Energy on the shoot. It is very useful to have the Stunt Players — not the Actors — go through the sequence to determine if it will work or not. Faster, cheaper and less prone to tears than having the Actors attempt it before they are fully trained and rehearsed. If the Stunt Crew show you the moves, you'll get an optimal understanding of the camera possibilities and the effect.

Stunt Coordinators will tell you that Directors and Producers often hesitate to try something new. This is understandable given the Time Pressure of Production, and it's also true that some Coordinators and Stunt Teams have a 'thing' that they are known for and gladly repeat from film to film. Again, use Pre-Production to explore, and even experiment, with the Stunt Coordinator and the team to find fresh approaches, because you certainly won't have time on-set.

Stunt Coordinators and Performers rightly get very upset at the cavalier attitude towards safety that some Directors and Producers display. When a Stunt Performer gets hurt on-set, nothing will drive the Coordinator and the team into righteous indignation more than hearing a Director say about their fallen comrade; *'I thought that was what he was getting paid for.'* Yet, Producers and Directors are quick to blame the Coordinator if an Actor should be hurt in any way — and that Coordinator will face the liability of lost time and money. Guess what? The Stunt Coordinator has the authority to stop production if what is being asked is unsafe due to lack of rehearsal, or if a Director insists on proceeding with something that is manifestly too dangerous. You heard me. Stop. Production.

In conclusion — here's what I believe are the salient points of working with a Stunt Coordinator and Stunt Performers.

Have a strong idea, or 'vision' as to what you want to accomplish with the action sequence. You might not know how to achieve it, but it is far better to admit that to yourself and accept the Coordinator's input and experience. Bring your references. Use them as starting points for your discussion.

Don't try out something 'new' on-set. Work out in Pre-Production the unique and astonishing sequence that will elevate the scene into 'must-see'. Trim it and rehearse it until you know exactly how much time it will take to shoot, and how it will be shot. Then adjust your Schedule to accommodate it. If the sequence is important enough to your film, then it behooves you to create the time it will take to shoot it. Shorten that less important dialogue scene. Axe that unimportant Establishing shot.

When you're young, fit and enthusiastic there's a temptation to feel invulnerable. Actors, Stunt Players and Directors are not immune to this. But movie sets are amongst the most dangerous of workplaces. When that danger is amplified with stunt work, caution must increase. Safety (and liability) is another first-class reason to bring an experienced Stunt Coordinator onto your set.

Sometimes that Stunt Coordinator is the Director himself. You might recall the final scene of Billy Wilder's 1950 film noir, *Sunset Blvd*. Gloria Swanson (as Norma Desmond) glides down a staircase, watched by a gaggle of onlookers including photographers, reporters and police officers. Swanson was 50 years old at the time — not ancient. She (correctly) felt that the scene would be more powerful if she didn't glance at her feet as she came down the steps. Wilder agreed, but he was worried. In his mind, the scene now included a stunt. Swanson suggested she go barefoot, so she could feel the steps. This wasn't enough for Wilder. He arranged male Extras at various points on the staircase, portraying photographers and reporters, with instructions to catch Swanson if she slipped and fell. You can briefly glimpse Swanson's bare feet for a few frames when she comes down the last steps — but you're not looking at her feet. You've been mesmerized by her unforgettable progress down that staircase and how not for a second does she behave 'naturally' and glance at her feet, but remains completely 'in character' as the faded silent movie star.

I hope you'll remember this little example of on-set safety, brought to us courtesy of one of the greatest Directors who ever lived. It is a Director's duty to protect his Actors and his Crew, no matter how slight or inconsequential the action is that they are required to make.

- *What about Dance Choreography?*

I'm no dancer. Filmed a lot of dancing though and I know what I like when I see it. Once again, you hire the Choreographer who understands what is required. Like many performing artists, Choreographers are perfectionist by nature. Getting to perfection tends to make these individuals very protective of their own 'vision' and 'process'. Always best to let the horse run free from the gate but be ready to pull them up if necessary.

Never make an assumption about a Choreographer based on their personality or physical appearance. Dancers are lithe, slim, bright-eyed and athletic. Choreographers may not be. Judge them on the results and watch how the Dancers react to them. (Although, when you attend a rehearsal run-through, you can be sure the Dancers will be very aware of that and will be watching you out of the corner of their eyes to see how *you're* reacting).

One of the best Choreographers I've had the privilege of working with was barely five feet tall, chain-smoked, never smiled and appeared completely unfit. Yet, those slender, super-fit Dancers hung on her every word and worked their hearts out to get the complex and rigorous performance that was being demanded of them.

Good Choreographers, in common with good Stunt Co-ordinators, will work 'to camera' with complete ease. Rely on the 'pros' to come up with solutions to your problems, instead of trying to 'show' them. That'll only end in tears and embarrassment — unless you happen to be a highly skilled Dancer or Stunt Performer in your own right.

CHAPTER ELEVEN

Post Notes

The best course you can take in Pre-Production regarding Post-Production is to actually consider it. These days, not many people do — unless they've got tricky Visual Effects to add to their film. Ignoring Post until it's time for Post is a mistake. We shall explore why, yet keep it brief so as to discuss the subject more fully in a further volume.

In those far-off days when actual film negative was used to make movies, the post-production process was taken more seriously. Calculations and limitations were made as to exactly how much film needed to be shot, and arrangements were made for the processing of the negative. Assistant Editors took over from Script Supervisors and laboriously 'logged' and organized all the material, first on paper, and then in physical space — the bins. It was necessary to find secure storage, rent film editing equipment, book screening rooms, cut the film and schedule the work flow between cutting room, dubbing theater and laboratory until the final Release Prints were 'struck'.

Today, the concerns have changed. The minimum requirement is to have a clear idea of how much storage you will need for the captured media and decide how powerful the edit suite needs to be. In 'Ultra-Low-Budget' and 'Micro-Budget' world, it's common that editing does not begin until Principal

Photography is wrapped — often because the Director is also the Editor. However, most Productions within our budget parameters have an Editorial team. That team prepares for the edit during Pre-Production and starts assembly-cutting during Principal Photography as the footage arrives from the set.

Having an Editor in close proximity, cutting yesterday's material, is an ideal situation for you because you and your Cinematographer can see how the shots fit together and the story unfolds. Problems the Editor might flag can easily be addressed if you still have immediate access to Actors, sets, locations, costumes and the like. Doing a 'pick-up' shot that will fix the problem when you have access to the elements is far better and much cheaper than having to reassemble them for a re-shoot months later.

For this reason, on large, well-organized shoots you often find that there is an Editor hard at work on-set. Or three Editors! But a Director's access to an Editor during Principal Photography is only part of the thinking. Time is just as important to a Producer as it is to a Director. The reason is Money and Marketing. 'Money' because the sooner a film is completed and sold, the sooner revenues start to flow, investments recouped, and interest charges stemmed. 'Marketing' because films are targeted to reach the marketplace at specific times or are intended to be submitted to particular festivals. That means deadlines — so there is no Time to waste waiting for a Director to finish shooting before beginning the Edit.

But even if you don't have an Editor present during shooting, or have no need to work towards a specific future deadline, at least try to use the Pre-Production phase to sit down for an hour and go through the script and some of the more complex sequences and shots you're thinking about. One of the most important services the Editor can perform for you in Pre-Production is to advise you what *not* to shoot. Editors have an ability to *edit* — so use their eyes and instincts to identify what you don't actually need. It's surprising how many scripts are full of moments that are unnecessary — moments that, if shot, will end up being discarded in any case. Similarly, a discussion with an Editor can help you establish your entry and exit points from specific scenes and help you feel the rhythm that needs to be established. If you don't have these kinds of discussions with an Editor during Pre-Production, then it becomes necessary to have them with yourself — and that can leave you unhappy and insecure. Substituting an Editor's input on these issues with input from your Writers, Producers, Script Supervisors or Cinematographers might give you answers, but seldom the same response you'd get from your Editor.

Let's move onto another area that nobody gets excited about until it is too late. Music. I wish I had a dollar for every Producer, Director and Screenwriter I've met who found it hard to accept that the music they so desperately want for their film is not going to be handed to them with the undying gratitude of the composer and publisher.

Music is incredibly expensive and the process of acquiring the right to use it can be extremely convoluted, with difficult legal obstacles to overcome. For that reason, to obtain permission to use even a few seconds of previously published music can take several months work.

Yes, you read that right.

This is why we have an important member of the team called the 'Music Supervisor'. It is also why you need to start getting choices regarding music underway as early as Pre-Production. If you're not talking to your Composer or Music Supervisor in Pre-Production, then don't expect to have all your music by the time you're doing the final mix of your movie.

First, a quick definition. In film, Music comes in two broad flavors; 'Source' and 'Score'. The latter is composed and recorded specifically to support and enhance the film (although previously recorded music that 'fits' the images is often treated as 'score'). 'Source' is music used within a scene or sequence and which has an identifiable 'source' — the D.J.s turntable, the diner jukebox, the car radio.

The biggest problem with music — especially popular recordings that tend to be used as 'source' for dance club scenes and the like — is that it always turns out to be much more expensive than anyone anticipated. (Which is another reason why it's completely redundant for screenwriters to 'suggest' music for specific scenes and include the artist and title in the script). On 'ULB' or 'Micro-Budget' productions, Producers will seek out musicians who want exposure — and are willing to negotiate something affordable... as in 'free'. This might work — until the artist's management hear about it and arrange a back-end deal that will take a satisfactory chunk out of the film's revenues. Alternatively, sticker-shocked Producers instruct a minion to go online and find a 'stock' music library, select a number of 'cues' for a fixed and minimal price, and ask the Editor to slot those cues into the movie. The term you'll hear for this is 'needle-drop' — based, presumably, on the fact that in olden days, before hipsters arrived to resuscitate the long-lost technology, music came to us via a needle scratching along the grooves of a flattened piece of vinyl.

Finding music from 'stock' libraries isn't a guarantee of creating an interesting and original soundtrack, but it's a cheap solution and 'cheap' is all it takes to satisfy some producers.

I'm not discussing music here merely to warn you to start thinking about your requirements early in the game — which, of course, is important — but because music is such a vital aspect of your film that you need to exercise creative control while you still can. Choosing a Composer is as important to your film as your choice of Cinematographer.

Happily, the mere announcement that a film is going to go into production is enough for you — the Director — to be flooded with emails from composers who'd like to work with you. The incredible competition amongst Composers for a finite number of film productions gives Producers a major advantage in the fee negotiation process. If you don't make your voice heard and your suggestions, preferences, creative visions and intuitions known, then someone else will take up the slack, and you'll be stuck with whatever choice is made for you.

Once the Composer is onboard, then a discussion of the script and of specific scenes that hold importance to you musically, is necessary. Composers need a great deal of time to do their best work, so if they're already part of the team before filming begins, you're giving the finished score its best chance.

If the 'Music Supervisor' is also briefed during Pre-Production, then it's quite possible that by the time you've wrapped production and started the edit there may be a substantial part of your 'Source' music secured and available to use as you cut.

I mention this optimal situation because so often the Composer and/or Music Supervisor don't get hired until picture is cut and 'locked'. This means they're doing their work while you're in audio post-production, and the short time-frame common in audio post (4 to 8 weeks generally) puts them under considerable pressure. It also means that your picture Editor will have used 'temporary' music to approximate the music that will ultimately be used. This leads to a dangerous situation called 'Temp Love' which — as we will learn in a forthcoming volume— is a love affair that ends in disappointment and disillusion when the actual, and available, licensed music is placed in the show.

Getting started 'musically' while you're in Pre-Production can lead to some very happy occurrences. Sometimes a song, or a theme, is presented to you which surpasses your expectation and engages your creative thinking. You begin to see how the music will play under the images you have yet to shoot — and that might be very useful in how you proceed into your Shot List, or how you might make a change in the script to match the rhythms and moods created by the music, be it 'Score' or 'Source'.

There are some Directors who, instead of relying on getting the actual music prior to shooting, find some music that inspires them, and which works for the effect they are going for. Some even go to the length of playing that music during shooting, to help the Actors and Crew understand the rhythm and pace. To my mind, this is as dangerous as using 'temp' music in the edit. The feel of a piece of music can never be entirely re-created with another piece of music. Never.

Disappointment lurks — unless you're Martin Scorsese and you can afford to license *Gimme Shelter* for the umpteenth time.

And so, to the third and final section of things to consider in Pre-Production regarding your Post-Production. This is the area that seems to conjure up the most fear and misunderstanding in filmmakers venturing into long-form projects for the first time. I speak of the nightmare known as; Visual Effects.

VFX might sound scary — but really, it's not. You Tube is packed with examples of how to achieve amazing visual tricks by practical means. And that's my first point. In pre-production you should examine if there is a 'practical' way to get the effect you want. Too many people skip over this stage and assume that a VFX artist sitting for a month in a dark room will save them the trouble. If Christopher Nolan can do 'zero gravity environments' for *Inception* (2010) in physical space, then perhaps by going the 'practical' route you'll arrive at something cool and amazing without spending your entire post production budget. Our cinematic forefathers, you will recall, amazed audiences for decades with 'practical visual effects' that seemed impossible — mostly done through camera placement or by building a specialized structure (in pre-production) that allowed them to work the magic. Harold Lloyd wasn't dangling 80' above Broadway in *Safety Last!* (1923), although the iconic photo of him clinging to a clock face appears to show exactly that. During pre-production, Lloyd and his team built a portion of a building façade (plywood and paint!) on the flat roof of an existing office building. The 'clock' attached to the scenic flats was designed to come free of its mounting, leaving Lloyd clinging to the 'hands' for dear life — (although if he had fallen, at most he might have sprained his ankle). But how did they get the angle from above Lloyd, giving a view of Broadway far below and making it appear to the audience that the camera was suspended high above the street? Simple. They built a second platform on the roof — a few feet 'forward' of the façade — and placed their camera on it.

So, think old-fashioned 'practical effect' first — and then add in modern technology to help the idea along. If you were shooting *Safety First!* today you might still build the façade, but there would be no need to build it on a roof. You could shoot it at ground level in a car park, and place green screen in your backgrounds, adding high angle footage shot from an existing downtown office block once you were safely in post.

The majority of visual special effects in 'Low Budget', 'ULB' and 'Micro-Budget' productions are simple and straightforward. Some you barely need to think twice about —muzzle flashes from the rubber firearms, blood spray from the bad guy getting shot in the head, explosions blowing out windows, flames leaping up walls. What you're doing in these examples is compositing image(s) over image. The principal preparation involved is in making sure that you have left 'room' for the VFX and that you are shooting in a way that doesn't cause problems with the composite. Here's an example from a movie of mine called *The Missing Link* (2018) showing a saber-tooth tiger racing past a group of cavemen.

There was minimal pre-production preparation other than the awareness that a wide shot was required with foreground and background information, and that the Actors would be directed to react. In this frame, only two of the five Actors are looking directly at the invisible saber-tooth — the others have an eyeline that incorrectly extends forward of the line of travel — but the moment goes by so fast the audience doesn't see the mistake, and the pre-production planning (such as it was) also included immediate cutaways to reaction shots to take the audience 'away' and into another moment.

Eyelines, and directing Actors who are trying to figure out where the 'composite image' is supposed to be, are your principal problem when working either with green screen or (as was the case with *The Missing Link*) by leaving 'room' for the added element — but that's a production issue.

However, once you start going beyond the 'simple' and start shooting for significant visual effects post work, your pre-production planning requirement increases. The above frame from *The Missing Link* sequence was shot on a locked down tripod — so that the compositor had a shake-free series of frames to deal with. But what if you need complex tracking or aerial shots? What if you are incorporating a stunt into the sequence? What if you need motion-capture of an actor so that the human form can be replaced, or modified with CGI? What if everything in the scene you are shooting doesn't physically exist? There's a number of essential first steps you need to take.

- Photograph, in detail, the chosen location or...
- Request the Art Dept to make a model of the studio set
- Prepare a basic storyboard
- Write a short description of your intention
- Discuss the shot(s) with your VFX supervisor/crew
- Relay the VFX requirements to Camera & Art Depts.

Further steps are to make sure that your Key Department Heads understand how the shot is going to be made and that the issues that affect their work are understood and followed.

- The Cinematographer to be fully briefed on the VFX requirements for shutter speed, tracking markers, etc.
- The Art Dept., made aware of the intended camera angles, set dressing requirements and any specialized set building issues or prop handling.
- The Stunt Coordinator briefed on the shot(s) and any issues of safety and/or required equipment to be noted.
- Costume and Make-Up Departments briefed on any use of green or blue screen (and how that will affect make-up and costume choices), plus issues of how the shot(s) might require adjustments to costume, or to hair, skin tone, or for specialized make-up choices.
- The VFX Supervisor (or a knowledgeable designated person) instructed to maintain a complete on-set record/log of each shot including all camera settings, camera position, lens height, distance from object/subject and the placement of lighting.
- The Script Supervisor informed of any required Background Plates that will be shot during production and made aware of correct eyeline intentions.

So, where is the nightmare that everyone keeps talking about? Well, the problems begin if a director does not follow through in pre-production by liaising with all the departments. Those problems are compounded if, during production, the director fails to oversee and support a viable working 'pipeline' into post-production.

When we talk of a VFX 'pipeline' we often take it to mean a process that occurs only in post-production when the elements that go into a final VFX shot are assembled, piece by piece. But the VFX 'pipeline' doesn't begin in post-production, it begins in pre-production. (Actually, it begins with the screenwriter if you think about it.) As director, (i) you're taking that germ of an idea from the script page and (ii) over-seeing it from infancy to 'concept', then (iii) shepherding the concept through various stages of 'pre-viz', (iv) briefing the production crew in liaison with the visual effects crew, (v) preparing for the correct and precise capture of the 'production elements', then (vi) controlling the direction in filming the required shots, (vii) checking and supervising delivery of those elements into post-production with a complete log of each element and (viii) continuing oversight of the visual effects work as the final shot is assembled.

Naturally, there's more. The breakdown of what happens in post-production would double or triple that list — but in terms of Selecting For Success you'll be good if you can check off (i) thru' (v).

CHAPTER TWELVE

Money Matters

Any serious business-person has to know how to read a Profit and Loss Statement. Similarly, if you are a serious filmmaker (and I'm not confining the term to people who 'produce' films, but also to those who 'create' them), you are at a real and dangerous disadvantage if you don't know how to read and understand a Film Production Budget.

Once you get beyond directing the kind of pictures that cost less than $250,000 to make, the likelihood of the production requiring a Completion Bond rises exponentially. And when there's a Completion Bond, the insurance company issuing the Bond will require the Director to 'sign off' on the Budget. By 'Signing Off', a Director is making a legal agreement that he or she has seen the entire proposed budget, has understood it and is willing and able to make the movie within the budget and schedule limitations.

In a previous chapter, I referred in passing to a Completion Bond and might have left you unsure of exactly what that is and how it works. Here's a fuller explanation;

When large amounts of money are involved in a commercial film project, investors get nervous. The bigger the dollar amounts, the more nervous they get. To allay their collective anxiety, a Producer will take out an insurance policy to cover the investors and the production company if something occurs to prevent the completion of the picture within the agreed time and budget.

Now, there are many things that can go wrong during film production — death, illness, bad weather to name a few — and, if you can afford it, all these things can be covered. One of the primary things that makes investors most anxious and fearful is a 'creative and artsy' personality (you) being given the freedom to spend their cash on something as insubstantial as words on a page and an undefined and nebulous 'vision'. In their eyes, Artists (and Directors are included in this category) are not-quite-right-in-the-head and — worse — tend to be fiscally irresponsible. To the 'Suits', a Director (especially a young and inexperienced one) is a risk equally capable of sinking the project as any other catastrophe. But, happily, they have a policy that takes care of problem Directors, dead Actors and the like —an insurance policy that guarantees the completion of the movie. A policy which insures that the film will be finished and made ready for sale— no matter what. The Completion Bond. An essential component if money is to be released and the project put into production. Which means you, dear artsy-crafty director, are now the responsibility of the insurance company.

And how does the Insurance Company regard you, you might ask? Not with any great respect or favor, and certainly not with awe and admiration. You are a liability, and you will remain a liability until the picture is ready to go to market. First, they want to be sure that you and your lead Actors are healthy enough to stay alive and able to work for the duration of the shoot. You will be required to take their medical examination. You can drop dead once the picture is done — but not now.

Next, they will want you to legally accept your responsibility to bring the film in on Time and on Budget. If you agree that the film can be shot in a specified number of days — they will hold you to that. You will be asked to 'sign off' on the Schedule, and in doing so you will have accepted that you will complete the agreed number of script pages per day. They'll want — and they will get — signed reports from the Assistant Director showing that you have indeed 'made the day'. Every day. If for some reason you fall behind, they will have no hesitation in speeding things up. The easiest way to do that is to replace you. Yes, they have the authority — and good luck getting more directing work when word spreads that you were taken off the show by a Bond Company.

Their other remedies might keep you on the picture, but it will be uncomfortable. They can bring on 'their' Director to supervise you. They can replace your Assistant Director with someone who will *not* allow you that extra take or set-up and who will drive your demoralized crew into the ground. They will harass your Producer who in turn will harass you. They will request scenes removed from the script to bring things back on schedule. They will deny you that super-expensive but oh-so-cool piece of equipment to do that amazing once-in-a-lifetime shot — because you're heading over budget and the shot will take too long to film. And that's just the start. Because if you're still a problem to them in Post-Production, they'll take over that too. Which means, 'their' picture editor, 'their' post supervisor, 'their' audio house, 'their' colorist, 'their' re-recordist. It's not going to be easy to put your 'A Film by —' credit on that picture, is it? Especially as the completed film might bear little resemblance to your original 'vision'. But hey, the investors are happy, or will be until the day the film tanks when the reviews call it a 'slapped together, unhinged, visionless piece of hack work.' Chapter 2's notes on how not to set yourself up for failure during the Scheduling process take on a different urgency, don't they?

Now that you understand how the Completion Bond company manages the aspect of Time, let's look at the other liability. Money. Here your responsibility is to assure the Insurers that (i) you have read and understood the Budget, (ii) that you will not go 'over-Budget' and that (iii) over-runs will be justified, reasonable and agreed before any additional costs are incurred. While this is reason enough to be able to 'read' a Budget, there is a further reason — to do with the Producer. You want to be able to know that what has been discussed, agreed and planned has been properly costed, and that there is enough room in the budget to shift available funds if needed.

I come from an area of filmmaking that was notorious for budgets that would appear to be solid and then, usually during shooting, would suddenly turn out to be wildly inaccurate. Music video production, back in the day, was the Wild West. It was not unusual for substantial parts of the budget to completely disappear without warning or be allocated to costs incurred elsewhere. Like exotic car showrooms, or the ski slopes of the Italian Alps. Not that it was always the fault of Producers. Directors too would make demands for items that hadn't been accounted for, increase their shooting ratio and eat up expensive film stock, push a shoot into costly over-time or spend weeks longer than planned in the edit room. In those days, any such cost over-runs would normally be deducted from the Director's fee, most often without their knowledge until it was too late and the video had been delivered — so it became necessary to understand exactly how much money had been allocated to each Department and make sure that the money was actually there. Today's environment is much more civilized, and I'm sure there are no Producers these days who regard the production funds as *their* money. I am equally certain that today's entrepreneurs do not subscribe to the old adage of making sure that they get *their* money first. But don't take chances; you have a fiduciary right to examine the Budget!

The more likely negative scenarios you'll encounter in the lower reaches of our budgetary parameters are a result of inaccuracy, optimism or that old bug-bear, the desire to please. When you combine all three traits, you'll have a serious problem

But first, understand that not all budgetary problems are the fault of nefarious Producers, incompetent Line Producers or uncaring executives who don't understand your needs. Problems can begin for producers as early as the development phase when they realize that the investors they are negotiating with have strict limitations on what they are prepared to risk. A budget that has been calculated at $365,000 and aimed at the 'Modified Low Budget' slot has to be trimmed down to 'Ultra Low Budget' because only $250,000 can be raised. The first measure is to revise all the SAG Performing Rates downwards and follow that with the Crew Rates. Further trimming then begins in each Department — sometimes with wild guesses; (*'We can get the same camera & lighting package for 50% less!'*) Sometimes with over-optimistic projections; (*'We don't need five days to build the space-ship set — budget for two!'*) Sometimes by lopping off entire chunks of the budget; (*'Let's take the Post-Production numbers out — we can do a second round of financing for Post when the time comes!'*). My favorite is; (*'Why do we have to have a Contingency of 5% of the entire budget? It doesn't make sense! If we're smart nothing is going to go wrong, so we won't need a Contingency account!'*).

Once the funding has been negotiated and agreed, and first monies have been drawn down so that work and hiring can begin, reality will begin to bite. All budgets, by nature, are estimates. Unless the budget that secured the financing was fair and accurate, any mistakes in those 'estimates' now begin to be revealed. The newly-appointed Line Producer or U.P.M. may discover that the Crew Rates previously budgeted are 20% less than the actual and current 'going rate', or that no line items have been created for location permitting or such forgettable issues as parking and overnight security. It's the tiny things that easily get missed in original budgeting and which add up with anxiety-inducing speed. Icepacks to stop the digital camera over-heating. Fuel for the tow generator. The cost of re-painting a stage cyclorama. Trash pickup and site cleaning. Additional walkie-talkies. Cellphone allowances. Additional Hair Stylists and Costume Assistants for that massive ballroom scene. AA and 9v Batteries for Production Sound. Travel costs and 'per diem' for the horse wrangler and his assistant.

Pre-production is a budgetary nightmare of Department Heads being told what is in the budget for them, their reaction to that information — and the Line Producer then being forced into a decision that will affect either the filmmaker's creativity or the budget limitations of another Department. It can turn into an endless tug-of-war. To pay for that desired piece of camera equipment and the operator, does the Line Producer take $1,000 from the Art Dept's budget, (leaving the Art Director to find a way to reduce essential Set Dressing or Prop Rentals), or does she skim that money out of Craft Service and Stage Facilities? (Making the Craft Service guy drop the idea of hiring an assistant — and boxing the Stage into eating $500 in fees they would normally charge for some 'additional service'.)

Somewhere in all this, you are going to be asked for decisions. Do you really need the detail you've outlined for a particular set? Can you and the Cinematographer have a rethink about the special lighting you've requested? Do you really need fifteen background performers when the original budget only had six? Is there any way we can shoot the car interior scene without using a process trailer? This is where the old joke comes from;

Q. *How many Line Producers does it take to change a light-bulb?*
A. *Does it have to be a light-bulb?*

I never met a Line Producer I didn't love. I mean, I really love those guys. Because I have compassion and empathy. But they must be tamed and domesticated. They must never be allowed to suggest that a small portion of your fee might cover the extra-ordinary and difficult demands you are making on the budget. '*Yes, yes*', you'll hear them say — they appreciate the importance of the shot and '*in normal circumstances*' they'd be the first in line to give you what you need, but you must understand how tight funds are… and they'd gladly get that special item for you if you would just meet them half-way! Ha! There is no such thing as 'half-way' — not with a Line Producer! 'Half-way' is their shorthand for 'All-the-way'! Respond politely. Wonder aloud if they would give up some of *their* fee, or if another Director can be found who can do the job on the cheap!

Your task is to become familiar with the kind of funding each department needs and check to see if there is (i) sufficient manpower in the department to do the type and amount of work you anticipate, (ii) if the correct equipment has been itemized with accurate costing and (iii) if the correct number of days when manpower and equipment is in use has been estimated. This is not as hard as it seems, given the amount of information available online. It's important to see where budget estimates are 'under' and if there is enough gentle 'padding' so that unexpected costs can be handled, and potential excess assigned elsewhere. The difficulty comes with items that are harder to check — such as legal and accounting fees. In those cases, just be on the lookout for anything that seems wildly unreasonable.

The Production Budget you will encounter has three parts; (i) Top Sheet, (ii) Account Level and (iii) Detail Level. For independent movies (rather than studio pictures) it should include everything — from the Development Phase through Pre-Production, the Production itself, Post-Production, Marketing and Delivery and all the Administrative matters like office rentals and business licenses, to Insurance, Legal and Accounting fees. Not every item budgeted may be totally accurate or foreseeable — but the more experienced the Producer's Unit, the closer those numbers will be to the actual figures.

160 | MARKUS INNOCENTI

PRELIMINARY DOLLAR BUDGET

Prep: 6 Weeks
Shoot: 7 Weeks (37 Days + 2 B Roll Days)
Post: 14 Weeks

Budget Date:
Exchange Rate:

US DOLLAR BUDGET

Acct#	Category Title	Page	Total
801-00	STORY & OTHER RIGHTS	1	$189,000
803-00	WRITING	1	$32,261
805-00	PRODUCER & STAFF	1	$706,239
807-00	DIRECTOR & STAFF	2	$180,442
809-00	TALENT	3	$651,619
	Total Fringes		$74,281
	Total Above-The-Line		**$1,833,842**
811-00	PRODUCTION STAFF	8	$443,749
813-00	CAMERA	11	$307,038
814-00	ART DEPARTMENT	13	$171,064
815-00	SET CONSTRUCTION	14	$154,560
816-00	SPECIAL EFFECTS	16	$173,250
817-00	SET OPERATIONS	16	$164,688
819-00	ELECTRICAL	17	$363,566
821-00	SET DRESSING	19	$399,137
823-00	ACTION PROPS	20	$66,031
825-00	PICT. VEH & ANIMALS	21	$56,035
829-00	EXTRA TALENT	21	$114,682
831-00	WARDROBE	22	$244,869
833-00	MAKEUP & HAIR	23	$98,210
835-00	SOUND	24	$79,288
837-00	LOCATION	25	$812,790
838-00	VIDEO TAPE	31	$22,485
839-00	TRANSPORTATION	31	$391,065
841-00	FILM & LAB	34	$29,808
845-00	FACILITY EXPENSES	34	$67,726
	Total Fringes		$158,602
	Total Production		**$4,318,643**
851-00	EDITING & PROJECTION	35	$217,147
852-00	VIDEO TAPE POST	36	$20,000
853-00	MUSIC	36	$149,350
855-00	SOUND (POST PRODUCTION)	36	$71,565
857-00	FILM, TAPE, & LIBRARY	37	$198,505
858-00	VISUAL EFFECTS	37	$50,000
859-00	TITLES & OPTICALS	37	$25,000
	Total Fringes		$10,362
	Total Post Production		**$741,929**
861-00	INSURANCE	38	$160,000
862-00	PUBLICITY	38	$16,931
865-00	GENERAL EXPENSES	38	$209,419
	Total Fringes		$0
	Total Other		**$386,350**
	Completion Bond 2.5%		$182,019
	Contingency - Capped		$500,000
	TOTAL ABOVE-THE-LINE		**$1,833,842**
	TOTAL BELOW-THE-LINE		**$5,446,922**
	TOTAL ABOVE & BELOW-THE-LINE		**$7,280,763**
	GRAND TOTAL		**$7,962,782**

The previous page has an example of a Top Sheet created in Movie Magic Budgeting showing the preliminary work-up for a $7.9m U.S. independent production shooting in Europe.

This might be the first time you've encountered the phrases 'Above-The-Line' and 'Below-The-Line'. It sounds like some kind of military-speak and in a sense that's exactly what it is. All those Accounts 'Above' the so-called 'Line' relate to the High Command. You're not supposed, nor will you be able, to look at them too closely if you haven't been given clearance. Here you will find all the figures, estimated and actual, relating to; (i) acquiring the script, (ii) compensating the Producer (including paying back the Development Costs), (iii) the fee and the perks negotiated with the Director and (iv) the expense of the Talent contracted to appear. Sometimes all the Talent is put 'ATL' and other times, perhaps to make the Sub-total seem less outlandish, only the 'Stars' appear 'ATL', the rest of the Cast being consigned 'Below-The-Line' in closer proximity to the Extras and Craft Service. Much like real-life.

You might have noticed that the example Top Sheet has accounts labelled 'Video Tape' and 'Video Tape Post'. That seems arcane, but many larger productions still shoot in 35mm or — more often — Super35mm, and 65mm film production is not unknown. 'Video Tape' covers all those transfers between production and laboratory. The terminology is being gradually replaced with labels like 'Media'.

Once you've studied 'ATL' and established that your fee has been properly entered, marveled at how the Producers have hidden the bulk of their compensation in 'development costs' and choked on your morning croissant when you worked out the hourly rate being offered to your Leading Actor, turn your attention 'Below-The-Line' to all the accounts relating to Production.

Let me quickly go through the points that, as a Director, would catch my attention. I have only seen this Top Sheet summary and was not privy to the Account or Detail Levels. The only other information I have is that this preliminary budget did not include the star attachment that pushed the final budget to a little over $10m.

801. (Story & Other Rights). This is where the screenwriting options and purchase is accounted for, along with securing all the rights to make the picture and contract fees.

803. (Writing). The amount looks like a 'Rewrite' or 'Polish' fee, not the Screenwriter's entire fee.

805. (Producer & Staff). At $700k this obviously includes all the development costs, the meetings and the contracts and the travel expenses. To be fair, Producers find it hard to give themselves exorbitant fees — studio executives and investors don't look kindly on that and Producers have to eke out an existence on very limited funds until movies are in successful distribution.

807. (Director & Staff). This looks like the kind of fee being paid to a 1st time director, and I wonder how much is allocated towards 'staff' and accommodation/travel given the overseas location.

809. (Talent). At $651,619 this looks "light" to me for a 37 days shoot with the kind of actors that a $7.9m production demands.

What's missing? How about Travel & Living? Nothing budgeted for flights and hotels? That would be the focus of my questions before I 'signed off' on the budget.

Turning to 'Below-The Line', a total of $4.31m seems comfortable. Obviously, as you did with the 'Talent', you check that you have everyone you need for all the days that you need them — and that all the 'Fringes' have been accounted for. Every budget template is slightly different. You might find in this case that Account 811 (Production Staff) includes not only the Line Producer, the U.PM. the Assistant Directors, Script

SELECTING FOR SUCCESS | 163

Supervisor and the Production Assistants — but also Craft Service, Catering and sometimes the Grips. If so, then $443k might be "light". Here, however, Account 817 (Set Operations), with an additional $173k, might contain some of those items. The point is, you have to look at both Accounts to see what has gone where, and for how much.

Account #813 (Camera) is always a hefty number and here it is a respectable $307k. But again, I raise an eyebrow. Cinematographers and their crews don't come cheap and once you add equipment the cost balloons. The figure here is one that I would examine closely before I was convinced that there was enough in the budget.

Remember I said that it was in the Art Dept., that padding occurs most grievously? One of the reasons this happens is that the entire Art Dept., is able to spread itself across the budget — with, in this instance, four separate Accounts. (#814, #815, #821, #823). Add it up and it's a total just shy of $800k. In our example, one of those accounts, #821 (Set Dressing), comes in at over 50% of monies allocated to the Art Dept. However, sometimes rough guidelines are useful. Typically, an Art Dept. will eat up about 10% of a budget — so the $800k total is in the right ballpark. I usually figure the Camera Dept at 5% — which is why I raised that eyebrow earlier. Eyebrows also get raised in this budget when I see Account #839 at $391k. Is that where all the Travel and Airfares went? And why is the Wardrobe Dept., coming in at $244k. Sounds like a lot of fabrication is required.

Further down, on this quick scan of the Top Sheet, my gaze falls on 'Post Production'. Post looks solid — with satisfying numbers for #851 (Editing & Projection) and #853 (Music). But Account #855 (Sound) seems "light" for a production at this level. 'Sound' is where the movie comes to life. $71,565 might seem to be sufficient, but has enough time been allocated? Or are 'Fast' and 'Cheap' going to be our watchwords?

Lastly, the 'Other'. Again, much can be hidden in General Expenses — and there are always some significant, and uncheckable, figures for items such as Accounting and Legal. The line item that catches my attention is #862 (Publicity). At just under $17k this seems insufficient to me, and I'd certainly question this figure and speak to the Producer to see what we'd be getting for such a small sum. After all, I want the world to know about our movie.

With some issues raising concern, a deeper dive into the Budget is required. The following examples will show how to take a deeper dive into a Production Budget, moving from 'Top Sheet' through 'Account Level' to Detail Level'. The following examples are from a project budgeted at $2m, but the general layout is similar to the previous budget.

Budgets are not completely standardized in format, but they contain the same information — the line items are often placed differently, numbering is changed, some budgets include accounts that others find unnecessary and omit, but if you can read one budget, you can read them all.

1900	Camera	$86,375
2000	Electrical	$56,508.
2100	Sound	$19,850

Above is an excerpt from another production's Budget Top Sheet (created in Gorilla™). This one has a different layout and dollar amount, and the minimal information given is a summary.

In the above example, please note that the Account Number for 'Electrical' is #2000 and the total allocated is $56,508.

We need to know what's involved in Account #2000 to arrive at the #56,508 total. So, we take a dive into the next layer of the Budget — the Account Level;

Alex in the Afternoons

Acct #	Category	Account Title		Total
	1902	1st Assistant Camera		$8,100
	1903	2nd Assistant Camera		$7,375
	1904	Digital Imaging Technician		$8,000
	1905	Camera Package		$44,000
			Sub Total	$86,375
2000	Electrical			
	2001	Gaffer		$8,568
	2002	Best Boy		$7,464.
	2003	Electrical Grip/Rigger		$12,835.
	2004	Lighting Package		$25,200
	2005	Box Rental		$1,440
	2006	Expendables		$1,000
			Sub Total	$56,508.

Account #2000 is the 'parent' Account for the Electrical Department. Within that account, the Gaffer is Line Item #2001, the Best Boy is Line Item #2002 and so on. Add all those Line Items together and the Sub Total for Account #2000 is $56,508 — which matches the figure in the Top Sheet for that Department.

This 'Account Level', which is one step deeper than the Top Sheet, has given us an overview of how that $56,508 has been budgeted. In addition to the crew, the equipment has its respective totals. So far, so good. But wait. Line Item #2003 is odd. Why is the Grip/Rigger being paid $5,000 more than the Best Boy? For an explanation we must take a deeper dive — all the way down to the 'Detail Level'...

...where we find the reason. The 'Detail Level' on the following page shows that for Line Item #2003 there are *two* Grip/Riggers, each being paid $30 less per day than the Best Boy. Notice how every Line Item shown in the 'Account Level' has been expanded in the 'Detail Level' to further explain how those totals were arrived at.

1905	Camera Package								
	Red Carbon Dragon 6K		$0	......	4/WEEK(S	1	......	$4,000	$16,000
	Arri Ultra Primes		$0	......	4/WEEK(S	5	......	$1,400	$28,000
									44,000
2000	Electrical								
	2001	Gaffer							
		Prep	$0	......	2/DAY(S)	1	......	$306	$612
		Shoot	$0	......	24/DAY(S)	1	......	$306	$7,344
		Wrap	$0	......	2/DAY(S)	1	......	$306	$612
									8,568
	2002	Best Boy							
		Prep	$0	......	2/DAY(S)	1	......	$276.	$552.
		Shoot	$0	......	24/DAY(S)	1	......	$276.	$6,635.
		Wrap	$0	......	1/DAY(S)	1	......	$276.	$276.
									7,465
	2003	Electrical Grip/Rigger							
		Prep	$0	......	1/DAY(S)	2	......	$246.	$493.
		Shoot	$0	......	24/DAY(S)	2	......	$246.	$11,848.
		Wrap	$0	......	1/DAY(S)	2	......	$246.	$493.
									12,836
	2004	Lighting Package							
		5-ton Grip & Lighting Truck	$0	......	4/WEEK(S	1	......	$4,500	$18,000
		Tow Generator	$0	......	4/WEEK(S	1	......	$1,500	$6,000
		Generator & Truck Fuel	$0	......	4/WEEK(S	1	......	$300	$1,200
									25,200
	2005	Box Rental							
		Box Rental	$0	......	24/DAY(S)	2	......	$30	$1,440
									1,440
	2006	Expendables							
		All Expendables	$0	......	1/FIXED	1	......	$1,000	$1,000

Further examination of #2000 Electrical reveals that the crew have been given either one or two 'Prep' days, twenty-four 'Shoot' days and, with the exception of the Gaffer, one 'Wrap' day. The Production has a 5-ton Grip & Lighting Truck and Tow Generator — for all 4 weeks of the shoot — with a budget for fuel. There's also a 'Box Rental' fee (aka 'Kit Rental)' for Gaffer and Best Boy — a little daily 'bump' for the use of their personal equipment. There's a healthy amount for consumable materials — the 'Expendables'.

That seems to be a considerable amount of detail. But is it? Do we know what equipment is on the 5-ton Truck? From a Director's perspective, it's helpful to know what you will have available. There's a lot of equipment on a 5-ton truck you may never need or use — but it's comforting to know it's there. What is uncomfortable is finding out on the shoot that the equipment you need has not been placed in the 'package'. You need to ask for a list of that 'package' before you 'sign off'.

As you peruse budgets, keep in mind that mistakes can be made that will take monies and allocate them in the wrong place. In this example, if you knew — for certain — that a full two weeks of this shoot would be on a sound-stage with full power... why do you need the Tow Generator for the entire shoot? The Line Producer may know something you don't — that the sound-stage is notorious for power outages — but it's worth checking and, in this instance, you could save $3,000 and put that money to work elsewhere.

Finally, it's useful to know that the Line Producer has allocated $1,000 to Electrical Expendables. This is padding. Sure, things might need replacing. But $1,000? Smile as you casually draw attention to it. Let your Line Producer know that you know what he did, and you know he knows you know it.

Or something like that.

CHAPTER THIRTEEN

The Bottom Line

It's intimidating, over-whelming and slightly dispiriting to look at a film production budget that exceeds the amount FEMA spends on hurricane relief. You might think that the previous chapter's budget examples were irrelevant to your own situation, perhaps because you don't have the track record to be entrusted with those budget levels yet, or maybe because such hefty sums are unrealistic for your current creative needs.

Years ago, there was a very useful and inspirational book called *Feature Filmmaking At Used Car Prices* (Penguin, 1988) in which author Rick Schmidt demonstrated how to make a movie on a shoestring. Many similar books and seminars have followed — and they're all true, then and now. Today's digital filmmaking has dramatically kept costs down, (particularly in post-production) and so, thirty years on from Rick Schmidt's book, it's not impossible for today's emerging filmmakers to produce a watchable film for the same hard cash total Mr. Schmidt proposed back then. Which I seem to recall was $6,000. You could buy a nice clean used Mercedes for that price back in those happy times. Remarkably, this weekend and next, you could spend the same $6,000 and shoot all the footage you need to spend the next three months in your bedroom cutting a full-length feature film suitable for streaming worldwide.

Given the creative and career advancing opportunities created by 'Micro-Budget' filmmaking, let's round out this book with the Budget for a hypothetical feature-length film of the sort that may very well be your entry point into the film business. I've capped this budget deliberately at the current average price of a 3-year old used Mercedes E-class. $34,010. The kind of film I'm considering could be a 'horror' movie, or arthouse drama, with no, or minimal, stunts. The cast — mostly youthful and unknown, perhaps with a cameo from a former 'name' of 'recognizable' talent. The shoot would be a Screen Actor's Guild Ultra-Low Budget production and all the cast would be paid the same rate. The non-union crew would also be paid the 'SAG-ULB' rate in line with the Actors, but without the Pension & Health Benefits. There would be $25/day bonus bumps for the majority of Department Heads. Transport, including vehicles used 'on film' would be provided by Cast and Crew, with the exception of the occasional specialty 'Picture Vehicle' and a rental truck for equipment. Post-production monies would not be included in the Budget at this point, because the Producer and Director intend to edit the movie themselves in the apartment they share in Koreatown, with music, visual effects, sound editorial and color grading provided by friends who are also aspiring filmmakers. For the nitty-gritty of Delivery items (such as Closed Captioning, Re-Recording and Digital Cinema Packages) they are relying on finding more investment — ditto for Marketing and Publicity expenses.

When working in the 'SAG-ULB' mode, and with a budget capped at $34,010, you'll understand that 'Micro-Budget' Producers will make choices that would never fly for productions at higher levels. Most of the time, this means accepting constraints and challenges that those working with higher budgets don't need to bother themselves with.

Here's what the Top Sheet might look like;

10/24/2018

TOP SHEET

Budget for: Alex in the Afternoons	Director:
Budget Name: Digital No Budget Feature	Producer:
Alex in the Afternoons Red Dog Logic PO Box 5301 North Hollywood, CA 91616	Production Manager:
	1st Assistant Director:
	Prepared by: Markus Innocenti: (818) XXX-XXXX

Acct #	Category Title	Total
	ABOVE-THE-LINE	
1000	Script	$115
1100	Producers Unit	$1,110
1200	Direction	$850
1300	Cast	$4,000
	Sub Total	6,075
	PRODUCTION	
1400	Production Staff	$1,350
1500	Extra Talent	$375
1600	Art Direction	$1,630
1700	Set Operations	$2,240
1800	Set Dressing & Props	$1,730
2000	Wardrobe	$2,300
2100	Make-up & Hair Dressing	$1,480
2200	Electrical	$4,465
2300	Camera	$4,153
2400	Sound	$2,770
2500	Transportation	$555
2600	Location Expenses	$2,152
	Sub Total	25,200
	POST PRODUCTION	
2700	Editorial	
2800	Music	
2900	Post Production Sound	

Alex in the Afternoons   10/24/2018

TOP SHEET

Acct #	Category Title	Sub Total	Total
	OTHER		
3000	Contingency		$500
3100	Insurance		$1,600
3200	General & Administrative Expenses		$635
		Sub Total	2,735
	PERCENTAGES		
	Contingency	$0	$0
	Overhead	$0	$0
	Insurance	$0	$0
	Completion Bond	$0	$0
	In-Kind		

Total Fringes
Sub Total Percentages $0
Grand Total $34,010

The criteria used in arriving at these numbers included;

- Shooting Schedule — 8 days. 10 hours/day.
- Range — Los Angeles 30-mile studio zone
- Interior Locations — 5.
- Exterior Locations — 4.
- Camera — Canon C300, Canon 28mm-70mm lens, Atmos Ninja Recorder, Sachtler Tripod & Fluid Head
- Lighting — 1-ton (Grip & Electrical) Truck Package
- Sound —Sennheiser 416 w/Boom, Wireless Lavaliers, Zoom H4n Recorder.
- Meals — Catered Lunch, Coffee, Water, Snacks

The cast for a 'Micro-Budget' production such as this has to be kept to a minimum. Here we've budgeted for 10, plus 5 background performers. Actually, background actors — or the lack of them — is often a problem in this level of production, so screenplays that don't require the frame to be filled out with bodies are always welcome.

- Principal Cast — 4
- Supporting Cast — 3
- Day Players — 3
- Extras — 5

The 12-person crew would be as follows— note how the crew members, including the Producer and Director, handle multiple duties;

- Director/1st A.D./Script Supervisor
- Producer/UPM/Location Manager
- Cinematographer/Operator/Media Manager
- 1st Assistant Camera/Camera Grip/Clapper
- Lighting Gaffer/Electrical Grip/Truck Driver
- Lighting Best Boy/Electrical Grip
- Production Sound Mixer/Boom Operator
- Art Director/Prop Master/Set Dresser
- Art Dept. Assistant/Painter/Swing Gang
- Key Costume/Wardrobe
- Key Make-Up & Hair
- Production Assistant/Craft Service/Grip

Here's some of the constraints being accepted by passionate and committed emerging filmmakers;

- The only people being properly compensated 'Above-The-Line' are the Cast, who receive the SAG rate with its 18% Pension & Health 'fringe' benefit.
- The Producer is also the U.P.M. and the Director acts as her own 1st A.D. and Continuity.
- The screenplay has been 'optioned' for $50, copyrighted at the Library of Congress and registered with the Writer's Guild of America (West).
- Some 'Department Heads' are working for a basic rate, $25 higher than the Cast. All others work for the same

rate as the actors, (minus the 'fringes') except the Production Assistant on $75/day. (He's a future Director).
- Bagel and Coffee Breakfast, Basic Craft Service and Lunch provided. (Lunches should be varied and include 'home-style' main items such as Lasagna and Salad, Meatloaf and Mashed Potatoes, Chicken Stir-Fry and Rice — so that crew and cast feel they've had a meal, not a snack or a picnic).
- An allowance available for gas and taxis as required (or requested).
- 8 locations budgeted, and Film Permits obtained.
- Insurance per a Producer's Production Package to include General Liability, Worker's Comp, Auto, and Riders for Rental House equipment packages
- Bookkeeping Service and a fixed Contingency (not a percentage of total) included.
- No Post-Production included in Budget — with the Producer and Director doing most of the work *gratis*, intending to raise further monies later.

All the above is dependent on a Producer's ability to negotiate, a crew's willingness to work hard for little cash reward and the goodwill of rental houses, authority figures, property owners and the like. Welcome to 'Micro-Budget'.

Let's imagine, as we have for the larger budget we examined previously, that you — the Director — did not create this Budget. It's not your job, nor is it your required expertise, to know all the numbers and calculations that went into our Top Sheet examples. Your task is to make sure that what you are intending to do has been properly factored into the budget and accounted for.

For the Cast Account that means turning to the Detail Sheet and confirming that the actors have been designated the correct number of days. The rate they are paid is between the Actor, the Producer and the Guild, but the amount of days they are required to work is something for you to check and confirm.

1300	Cast							
	1301	Lead Actors						
		Role of Alexandra	$180	------	8/DAY(S)	1	------	$125	$1,000
		Role of Belinda	$135	------	6/DAY(S)	1	------	$125	$750
		Role of Charlie	$112.	------	5/DAY(S)	1	------	$125	$625
		Role of David	$90	------	4/DAY(S)	1	------	$125	$500
									2,875
	1302	Supporting Cast						
		Alfred	$22.	------	1/DAY(S)	1	------	$125	$125
		Bela	$45	------	2/DAY(S)	1	------	$125	$250
		Chaney	$67.	------	3/DAY(S)	1	------	$125	$375
									750
	1303	Day Players						
		Charlie's Boss	$22.	------	1/DAY(S)	1	------	$125	$125
		Alexandra's Mom	$22.	------	1/DAY(S)	1	------	$125	$125
		Man in Orchard	$22.	------	1/DAY(S)	1	------	$125	$125

The 'Detail Level' example above of Acct. #1300 (Cast) shows how Line Items within the account are broken down. In this case, #1301 holds the Leading Actors, with #1302 for Supporting Cast and #1303 for the Day Players. Each character is given their own Line. This is a 'SAG-ULB' production. The number to the immediate right of the character name is the Screen Actors Guild 'fringe' — a percentage of the Performer's Daily Rate that the Producer contributes to SAG Pension & Health benefits. (Note that there could be further 'fringes' — various payroll taxes and fees — but they are placed in a different account). After the 'fringes' comes the total Time the actor will be required/budgeted for. The next column indicates how many units are being budgeted, (1 Actor, in this case). Then comes the Daily Rate to be paid, and the Total.

In terms of crewing, you need to make sure that each department has the manpower they require to do the job you're going to ask them to perform. If MUAH (#2100) shows a single Key Make-Up Artist for the entire shoot, that might be fine. But if someone has forgotten that Day 7 requires 5 Zombies in full make-up all day long, then that Make-Up Artist needs an Assistant or two on the day.

2100	Make-up & Hair Dressing							
	2101	Key Make-Up Artist						
		Shoot	$0	------	8/DAY(S)	1	------	$150	$1,200
									1,200
	2102	Purchases						
		Zombie FX Make-Up	$0	------	8/DAY(S)	1	------	$15	$120
									120
	2103	Kit Rental						
		Kit Rental	$0	------	8/DAY(S)	1	------	$20	$160
									160

If that request is refused due to 'budget restrictions' then Day 7 is going to be a nightmare of waiting for those Zombies to come out of Make-Up and onto your set.

You need a 'trade-off' — unless you have a Key MUAH who swears on his mother's life that he can get all 5 Zombies in front of the camera whenever you need them.

If a 'trade-off' is required, make a mental note and keep alert for an account item that can be reduced or eliminated and free up enough cash to pay for a day's worth of Assistant MUAH.

In these circumstances I head first to the Art Department account. I know they're hiding something in there — probably enough to get my Assistant MUAH.

1500	Extra Talent							
	1501 Extras							
	Zombies	$0	------	1/DAY(S)	5	------	$75	$375
								375
1600	Art Direction							
	1601 Art Director							
	Prep	$0	------	2/DAY(S)	1	------	$100	$200
	Shoot	$0	------	8/DAY(S)	1	------	$150	$1,200
								1,400
	1602 Set Painting							
	Chromakey Paint (Green)	$0	------	2/GALS	1	------	$115	$230
								230

Let's see. #1602. Two gallons of Chromakey Green Paint budgeted at $230? I don't think so! Just the kind of item that seems important enough to intimidate a Producer and prevent him from asking questions. Quick research and calculation required. A quart of Chroma Green will cover 300 square feet and costs $28.75 including tax. The wall area we need painted is 20' by 15'. By some rare coincidence that's.... 300 square feet! The amount of paint budgeted at the Art Dept's request would paint the area 8 times. Let's re-budget for a single quart can and a spare and, hey — why not? — round it up to $30 a quart. $60 total. Which means we've just liberated $170. I think we got ourselves an Assistant MUAH.

Yes, the Art Director will complain and say that she needs two gallons for 'proper coverage' of the area, for re-painting and for touching up, or maybe the Director will ask her to paint a larger area, and aren't we forgetting the floor has to be painted too? The point is, you need $125 to pay the Assistant MUAH for one day. Your Producer can simply adjust the budget — releasing that money to MUAH so they can hire the Assistant — and reduce the paint line item to $105. More than enough for 3 quarts.

There's a multitude of places where money is assigned so that Department Heads and Producers can sleep easy knowing they have some padding. It takes time to learn them all but with your knowledge of what you actually need, and with pricing information you can easily glean from the internet, you should be able to suggest adjustments that will give you some comfort. Bear in mind that some line items *legitimately* require 'padding' because the Producer might not know until the last moment how much is actually going to be charged. Production Insurance, for example, is an area where information tends to come in at the last moment. As are final rates for hotels and flights.

The most egregious problem, of course, is a Producer who under-estimates everything either through ignorance, optimism or a desire to please somebody. If that results in a finite amount of money raised which doesn't meet the needs of the production, there's seldom a way of going back and saying to the funder, *"Hey, we made a small mistake in our calculations. Can we have another 20% so that we can do this thing?"* Nope. You will be forced into cutting your expectations. This might mean losing crew members, axing a location, reducing your shooting schedule, saying goodbye to that sweet piece of gear, reducing your post budget and, in extreme circumstances, giving up your fee.

Of course, the first thing that *ought* to go is the compensation being offered to whoever put the production into the mess with their ridiculous budgeting — but that never happens. In the filmmaking process — as the old truism states — the first stage of 'wild enthusiasm' soon gives way to 'dejection, disillusion and confusion', and is swiftly followed, in rapid succession, with the 'blame game' — 'disgrace and punishment of innocent parties' and the rewarding of the actual criminals with 'promotion and praise'.

Grit your teeth and learn to deal with it — and it will change you into a harder, wiser, more effective director.

CHAPTER FOURTEEN

The Last Word

The principal point of your job in Pre-Production is to set yourself, and the movie you are making, up for success. Do not allow anyone to set you up for failure, least of all yourself.

They may not be doing so intentionally, but sometimes a Producer or Department Head will suggest something to you because it is the easiest way to get you what they think you want. Examine all suggestions very carefully and make sure you've communicated exactly what you need, or you'll get a nasty surprise on the set.

Here's a droll little war-story for you. On my debut theatrical feature, I wanted to do a shot from high up in a tree while Sir Christopher Lee stood beneath looking up. The tree itself played an important part in the plot, so I wanted to use this moment to show the audience how tall and grand the tree was.

I asked the Production Manager to get me a 'cherry picker' for the shot — meaning a hydraulic Boom Lift that could extend around 20', give me the height I wanted and with a rock-steady platform I could put the 35mm Moviecam Super-America and its operator on. But I forgot that my American production terminology might be misunderstood on a foreign location. On the day of the shoot, I got to the point when the next set-up was going to be the HI-ANGLE tree shot. I asked my 1st A.D. where the 'cherry picker' was — and she got on her walkie. A few minutes later I heard this 'putt-putt' sound and looked around. Approaching were a couple of farm workers. They were steering some kind of three-wheeled agricultural rig powered by a 2-stroke engine. I stared at it. The farm workers looked mighty pleased with themselves. Turned out I was getting an 'actual' cherry picker. As used in cherry orchards. Full-extended reach – 8 feet. Stability – zero. Plan B? I went for a LO-ANGLE, with Sir Chris's head and shoulders in the bottom of frame and as much of the tree towering above him as I could get in the shot. Not what I wanted, but it's what ended up in the release print.

Recalling my first feature brings back some uncomfortable pre-production memories. I don't want to alarm you unduly, but if you're an 'emerging filmmaker' and not a 'known' quantity as yet, then accept this merely as a friendly word — one Director to another — regarding something to bear in mind during those heady days of Pre-Production.

- *Don't assume that, because you've been hired as the Director, you will still be the Director when filming starts.*

Many things can unseat you between the First Week of Pre-Production and the Start of Principal Photography. Sam Fuller once said; *'A Film is a Battleground'*. And the fight begins the day you are hired.

Your Producer has already made his mind up about you, and 'sold' you to his financial backers. If you are demonstrating your competence in the 'selection' process, and remaining respectful of your Producer, there shouldn't be a problem — unless a bigger Star and bigger Budget suddenly become possible and with that, the need for a better-known Director. With that hurdle overcome, you might think you can relax and get on with the job, but the battle may only have just begun. The next likely 'problem' is this. Everyone thinks they could write a blockbuster screenplay or best-selling novel. Many more believe their life mission is to direct. When a 'first-time' Director is brought onto a show all the 'old hands' who have worked with the Producer in the past will assume (perhaps rightly) that they could do a better job and that they should have been considered. The Producer might have been making vague promises to them for years, promises that were never intended to be kept – it's an ugly facet of the grease that keeps Producer/Key Creative relationships going. And now, along comes a production with a novice Director. That's a bitter pill for those who feel that it's their turn. You can be sure there'll be some hard lobbying for the Director's seat and every trick in the book will be used to convince the Producer that hiring you was a mistake that can be easily rectified by giving the directing reins to *them*.

So, without descending into bunker-mentality paranoia, be aware of the possibility that the Cinematographer, Editor, Line Producer, Assistant Director, Writer and Actors currently smiling at you and nodding at everything you say, may be fighting behind the scenes to get their chance to direct the show – relying on their established relationship with the Producer.

Be kind to them and realize that your intense preparation in Pre-Production, along with the clarity and detail you bring to the project, will take the wind out of their outrage, and soon they'll settle down and focus on their jobs.

The other side of this coin that you can rely on? A Producer will always back a 'first-time' Director who has some proven gift that can be exploited. Not least because it keeps his key crew exactly where he wants them.

Eager and hungry.

My earlier mention of Sam Fuller's remark that *'Film is a Battlefield'* leads me to make a remark of mine own…

- *You're Gonna Need An Army. <u>Your</u> Army.*

Think of making a film like playing a very lengthy and exhausting game of Chess. You have an army of pieces to move your strategy forward, in the hope of taking the glittering prize of a victory that, at any moment, could be snatched away. The strength of your pieces and how they are used becomes vital.

In film, it's very, very hard to be a one-man band. Even certifiable geniuses like Orson Welles found it nigh impossible. Not because Welles couldn't do the jobs of Producer, Writer, Director, Star — but because convincing the people with the money that he could was hard. With all due respect to his collaborators, Welles did not have a team that quite compared to his level. Thus, he looked alone. To investors, 'alone' means vulnerable. 'Vulnerable' means risky. 'Risky' means — 'take a hike'.

Unless you're the type of personality that just can't get along with the people you work with then it behooves you to use the selection process whenever you get a directing assignment to build your future army. But remember my harshest rule. There is no room for passengers once you get beyond the 'Hey, kids! Let's-rent-a-barn-and-make-a movie!' level of filmmaking. Unless the person you are intending to collaborate with has genuine talent, you can't help them become successful by selecting them for a job on a professional production. Reaching down to pull someone up is a profoundly decent thing to do, and perhaps it's a moral responsibility. But it's fraught with risk. The risk of being pulled back down yourself. You're not required to save the world and help the less fortunate. You are required to direct a picture so well that your career takes off into the stratosphere. If you are about to embark on the most important project of your career and you're thinking of hiring your one-credit friend who wants to be a

SELECTING FOR SUCCESS | 183

Production Designer/Make-up Artist/ Cinematographer/Producer — I have one word for you.

Don't.

No army? Nobody on your team? Nobody at a higher level backing you up? Nobody with known talent committed to working with you? Then, guess what? At this moment you're still… nobody.

- *Thanks a lot. Got any other suggestions?*

At minimum, your early career will need three of the following — but try to get the whole deck.

A young, thrusting Producer, smart enough to know how to keep his mouth shut and listen to the old dogs when that moment comes.

A cutting-edge, emerging Cinematographer (if young), or a wise, older D.P., with solid credits who can shoot fast.

A Star. Not a TV Star, an Actual International Movie Star who thinks you're amusing, smart and fun.

Another Star. This one could be forgotten about, and due for re-discovery — but a Real Star.

A good selection of Character Actors — but, careful. You need ones that make people smile (not yawn) when they figure out what movie they last saw them in.

A Writer or Writing Team. Smart, snappy, pitch-ready — most important? They 'get' you.

An Editor. Preferably old, wise and experienced. If young — then ambitious, confident and connected. Track record required.

A Composer or Composing Team. Young 'hip and happening' is okay but 'seasoned' is much, much better.

An Art Director. This is the one everyone forgets about.

A Development Financier. Rich Uncles, please apply.

An older Veteran Producer who actually has a career, an office, a telephone and a poster on the wall behind him of his latest movie. Which should have been produced in the current decade.

A Manager. 90% of them are not even a tenth as important or knowledgeable as they think they are. Remember that.

An Entertainment Lawyer. Rent them like the whores they are. Not marriage material.

A Big Talent Agency. Yeah, bottom of the list. Their agents will need to send gifts before you take their calls.

Although the above list is a little glib, I'm not being flippant when I say that your career depends very much upon the people you associate and surround yourself with. I'm going to return to this topic in the last book of the series, *Merchants In The House Of Film*, because it is extremely hard to launch a meaningful career unless you have the support and confidence of people who believe in you. There is nothing more important for a talented filmmaker to have than an equally talented producer who is able to convince the mighty and the powerful that you are the real deal.

I hope these pages have given you an understanding that good preparation sets you up for success and gives you advance warning of the potential for failure.

As I mentioned in the conclusion of *Decoding The Script*, in many respects, despite all the collaboration on offer, you're very much alone when you work as a Director. You have to protect yourself — and the project — not only in terms of your creativity and personal 'vision', but also from a quagmire of bad choices resulting from the ambitious expectations of others.

Selecting For Success has been about protecting the project, and your career, through your detailed preparations. There is nothing worse than a Director who is unprepared. That said, there are some Directors who feel that their creativity mustn't be constrained. They deliberately come onto a set without being fully prepared because they want to feel liberated from rigid plans. They want to freely express their creativity without the restraints of having to follow a scheme.

To some extent — fair enough. But it's an expensive risk to take, not just in terms of budgetary cost and time overruns — but also in human energy. The energy of your Crew whose job is to follow your lead, and the energy of your Actors who, for the most part, want to be directed with clarity and economy.

I have spent many hours of my life working under the direction of the Precious Few, those self-proclaimed geniuses who want to react to the 'moment'. The problem is that the geniuses spend an inordinate amount of time trying to figure out what to do next. The crew has to hang about and wait while hands that have never done a hard day's work are used to make 'frames'. Hours pass while monitors are consulted, arms waved about, scripts studied as if for the first time, and mirrors gazed into. Very often Precious Director will start to set something up, only to abandon the idea because a problem arises that they did not, at first, take into account. At that point they get tetchy and start apportioning blame amongst the innocent. Having wasted everybody's time, and depleted Actor and Crew energy, they eventually come up with a solution — having irritably ignored mild remonstration and hesitant suggestion from Key Department Heads. Usually it's a solution that everyone else on the set can clearly see is going to end up on the proverbial cutting room floor.

If you work on enough shoots, you'll run across Precious Director sooner or later. Who is Precious? The Director who comes onto the set in the morning, having declined to visit the studio during the pre-light and pre-build, and angrily expresses astonishment that the set is the wrong color, the door is in the wrong place, the set-dressing is not contemporary enough and the lighting looks "too bright". The same Director who will go to the Producer and complain that the Crew has got everything wrong and is not respecting their much-vaunted 'vision'. (This is the primary reason why I hate the word 'vision' but it's hard to find another word to use when discussing film direction and, believe me, I've checked the thesaurus).

Precious is the Director just bursting to use a particular and complex piece of hardware to get some Vastly Important Shot. Having wasted half a day getting the equipment into the right position, and realizing that time has run out, a shot is then executed that is almost entirely meaningless and which, on-screen, will probably last no more than five seconds — even if it makes it into the final cut.

I'm being absolutely serious about Precious Director. Before I became a director myself, I spent many years working with Directors who could actually direct — and with a minority that simply couldn't but had managed to convince the Suits that they were the real deal. I learnt more about directing from the Precious Ones than I did from the Directors that actually knew what they were doing. Without exception, the Directors who failed were, despite their 'genius' label and staggering self-belief, universally unprepared for the day's work. They seemed to believe that being a Director meant that the content of their feeble brains would automatically be downloaded to the underlings who served them. You could see them wonder, as they spun in the wind, why the serfs were not comprehending their 'vision' and why everything wasn't just falling into place in the way they felt entitled to.

- *Why, oh why? The humanity! Why?*

Because, beyond deciding what T-shirt and baseball cap combo to wear for the shoot, Precious Director hadn't actually figured anything out in Pre-Production is 'why'.

And saddest of all, these self-styled *auteurs* arrived in post-production and made life impossible for another group of professional filmmakers — the Editors, the Visual Effects teams, the Sound Mixing crews. The Precious Few sit in edit rooms and dubbing theaters in the world's film capitals and wonder why their film isn't comparing favorably with whatever standard has fired their fevered and delusional imagination. What Precious is never told — and it's unfortunate, because they have to find a way to learn it on their own — is that if their film hasn't been planned as carefully as the world-class cinema they compare and aspire to, the chances are that a silk purse cannot be made out of the sow's ear they dumped into the post-production process. Oh, Precious will try to make pigs fly — and will waste the time, dollars and patience of all who are valiantly trying to elevate the inadequate footage into something that will keep the audience in their seats until the end credits. But, ultimately, it won't work.

There are many Directors who have reached the end of the entire process — maintained their confident, borderline arrogant, self-belief from Day One of Pre-Production right through to the Final Day of Post-Production — and have then seen their completed film screened uninterrupted and under ideal conditions. This screening is the first time they will have watched the film in its entirety with its finished soundtrack. For the first time, they are watching the film *as an audience will see it*.

And they realize, to their discomfort, that (i) it doesn't compare to the film they had in their head when they first read the script, (ii) it certainly doesn't belong in the pantheon of the great films that inspired and convinced them to become

Directors in the first place and (iii) it fails on the minimal level of having any kind of 'signature' that points to this being a unique work made by an *artist*. That's a very, very tough realization to have. An epiphany that can crush a fragile ego. Watching your film *as an audience will see it*, is sometimes a brutal and chastening experience.

So, cast your mind back, lowly crew member, to that moment during production when something went wrong or didn't quite work, and you heard Precious declare; *'Don't worry, we'll fix it in post'*. Well, it's true. Just about anything can be fixed in post. But when you hear the immortal *'we'll fix it in post'* line being delivered, just remember that the sub-text is this;

- *A problem has been encountered that has not been anticipated or prepared for.*

Later in The Filmmakers Art series, I'm going to talk a great deal about Post-Production — so there'll be an opportunity to examine the things you will need to be more fully aware of before you begin shooting. Most films are made in such a way that the work done in post unifies and makes understandable the disparate elements gathered in production. But that's not 'fixing it in post'. That's shooting it *for* post. And whenever you shoot things *for* post, you have to be even more prepared than usual.

So, what happens when Precious brings footage that has been shot without proper preparation or consideration into Post-Production? Let us count just a few of the Highways into Hell.

Missing or Unusable Shots:

Precious was so busy working out what to do next, he ran out of time, so (i) he never got the vital CLOSE-UP of the all-important line — it only exists in a lazily composed MASTER shot. (ii) Precious was so irritated by the crew's inability to keep up with 'his' speed that he also forgot all the REVERSE REACTION/CUTAWAY/INSERT/ESTABLISHING shots his Editor now desperately needs. (iii) Precious got a bit bored with the whole thing because it turns out that directing is tiring, so he decided not to bother with further set-ups once he'd done a few, and it was easier to just shoot a couple of takes and then move on. Besides, the Producer complimented him on how fast he was working. The fact that he only got one take of an important shot, which turns out isn't in focus, is not his problem — it's the Cinematographer's — and the Editor will just have to fix it with that 'focus sharpening thing' in the computer.

Missing, or Bad Quality, Audio:

Precious lost patience with the Sound Mixer's request for more time to place microphones properly, so (i) an entire side of a long conversation is 'lost' in heavy ambient sound. (ii) Despite the poor quality of the production dialogue (entirely due to Precious not checking the recording and/or failing to accommodate the Production Sound Mixer), Precious insists that Post-Production ADR is 'artificial' and won't allow the replacement dialogue to be added during re-recording. (iii) There was a mirror on the set so Precious wasn't really paying attention to what the Actors were saying during many of the takes. He didn't notice if they dropped a line or said something incorrectly. The Script Supervisor did, and pointed this out, but this only irritated Precious. He ignored the warnings, claiming they could be fixed in post. It turns out that they *can* be fixed in post — by using expensively recorded ADR replacement lines. But, as we've learned, Precious simply hates ADR and demands that the team find another way to fix the problems. With nowhere to run or to hide, the Post Crew apply the ultimate 'fix'. The picture is 'unlocked', the audio team stands down, and the picture Editor recuts sequences to avoid the unusable dialogue or the out-of-focus shot. The audio team reassembles, and re-conforms the picture back into sync. As far as the audience is concerned — they will never notice there had ever been a problem, but Precious has a sulk because the unusable shot/dialogue is no longer part of his 'masterpiece'.

Unsuitable VFX Footage:

Precious needed a vacation before production began, and upon his return he was obliged to take many important meetings in fashionable restaurants. He never had time to discuss the VFX with a Visual Effects Supervisor. He went so far as to tell the Producer that he was experienced in VFX and didn't need an on-set VFX Supervisor. The Producer made the mistake of trusting Precious. As a result, (i) the various Green Screen footage, background plates and Motion Capture media has become extremely difficult (and expensive) to work with. (ii) The VFX post team were improperly briefed and so could not give Precious their exact requirements — not that he was listening to them in any case (iii) Precious said he'd keep field-notes, but he got bored and distracted and so the VFX team has been handed incomplete notes and has no reference for the captured media. (iv) Cost overruns are now inevitable.

Music Nightmares:

Precious insisted on his 'own' composer for the score. This turned out to be (i) a friend who had never scored a motion picture before. (ii) Because he likes music, has eclectic Spotify playlists and contacts with famous musicians who will provide all the 'source' music for free, Precious convinced the Producer that he could take on the role of 'Music Supervisor'. Unfortunately, the famous musicians have managers and publishers who have very definite ideas on how much the sync licenses will cost. They also have lawyers who want to spend three or four months making sure the license clearance contracts are good. Precious isn't comfortable with lawyers and managers. The Producer quietly delegates the job to a real Music Supervisor and vows never to work with Precious again. But he probably will, because Hollywood's like that.

It is time now to bid you 'adieu' and 'au revoir' as this concludes the second volume of *The Filmmaker's Art*. You may have thought that there isn't a whole lot of 'Art' in the Pre-Production process, but I hope *Selecting For Success* has given you an understanding that to be truly creative, in-depth preparation is vital.

True, there's a fine line between being properly prepared and over-prepared. Don't let your Pre-Production take the fun and the sense of possibility out of your work. There's joy and real creativity in trying something that just occurs to you. Being properly prepped, and having a plan, will give you the extra time you'll need to go down a side-road and explore.

Just don't be 'Precious' about it. Please.

ABOUT THE AUTHOR

Photo Credit: Hannah Cowley Rath

Markus Innocenti tries not think too much about the sad fact that Orson Welles spent 95% of his professional life trying to fund films and only 5% actually making them. He's directed four feature films, a documentary or two, a handful of commercials and some music videos.
His first screenplay was produced. Which was nice.

ATTRIBUTIONS & ACKNOWLEDGEMENTS

Ingmar Bergman quote excerpted from "Talking With Ingmar Bergman" Edited by G. William Jones, Southern University Press, 1983

I would like to express my appreciation to artist Katie Maratta for graciously allowing me to include her work 'Silent Pictures: How Directors Think The Universe Is', first published in the Calendar Section of The Los Angeles Times, Jan 28th, 2001

Still frame from "The Missing Link" (2018) courtesy of The Two-Bit Picture Show Company, Producers Michael King, Dan Sheldon

AUTHOR LINKS & FREE DOWNLOADS

Free downloads of material discussed in the books, along with full-color versions of images featured, can be accessed on my website.
Navigate to; Series>The Filmmaker's Art>Media

https://www.markusinnocenti.com/

Further pics and info can be found on the Red Dog Logic Tumbler blog.

http://reddoglogic.tumblr.com/

THE FILMMAKER'S ART SERIES

Currently Available...

DECODING THE SCRIPT
Directors read scripts in ways that others don't, but the Clues are there for everyone to see once they understand how to 'decode'.

SELECTING FOR SUCCESS
Failure to properly prepare for production leads to bad choices and bad films — and sometimes good intentions have unfortunate results.

SHOOTING THE LIST
The Shot List is the Director's roadmap. This book discusses why it is important to have a List, and how to construct one.

Future Volumes... (Titles and Content Not Contractual)

EYE OF A POET
Working with a Director of Photography, understanding basics of Composition, Lighting and Lenses, and the use of Motion and Movement.

ACTORS ON SET
A deep dive into the challenges and rewards of the collaboration between Actors and Directors.

CUTTING FOR KEEPS
Delivering the movie you wanted to make.

MERCHANTS IN THE HOUSE OF FILM
An insider's look at the industry and the career path you might take.

www.ingramcontent.com/pod-product-compliance
Lightning Source LLC
Chambersburg PA
CBHW071457040426
42444CB00008B/1380